BUMBLING THROUGH BORNEO

WRITTEN AND ILLUSTRATED BY
TOM SCHMIDT

WHAT OTHER READERS ARE SAYING ABOUT THE
BUMBLING TRAVELLER™ ADVENTURE SERIES:

"*Bumbling Through Sumatra* is funny, beautiful and informative. It conveys the local colors, describes the local communities with respect, and highlights environmental problems. It is new kind of travelling book which I recommend everyone to read, not only us former backpackers. I am eagerly waiting for the third book in the series."
-- **Mahmud Bangkaru, Founder, Yayasan Pulau Banyak (Foundation), Aceh**

"The only problem with *Bumbling Through Sumatra* is deciding whether to read the cracker of an adventure story or meandering over to the pages about piracy, orangutans or what causes a tsunami. The thing is those pages are just as engaging as the story. Devious man that Tom Schmidt... makes you learn stuff without your realising it."
-- **Joan Lau, Managing Editor, The Malaysian Insider**

"[*Bumbling Through Borneo* is] a travel book with a difference. Engagingly written and amusingly illustrated in comic book-style format, it combines a rollicking backpacker's adventure tale in the heart of Southeast Asia's disappearing jungles with an increasingly serious environmental message."
-- **South China Morning Post**

"*Bumbling Through Borneo* is a classic Backpacker Yarn. Enlightening regional info digressions from the travelers' tale highlight environmental devastation of a global treasure. Splendid comic book-style ink drawings illustrate the journey. Old travelers will chuckle at the wanderers' jams, and young ones will be inspired to hit the road."
-- **Judith Mayer, Coordinator, The Borneo Project**

"This book is a unique approach to share stories of disappearing plants, animals, lands and waters local people need to survive. A good blend of a tourist rough guide, conservation notes and a comic book. A good treat for eyes and mind."
-- **Ahmad Fuadi, Director of Communications, The Nature Conservancy - Indonesia**

"Encouraging anyone to have an interest in exploration and the natural world can never be a bad thing, so *Bumbling Through Borneo*, which is set to entertain while imparting information, is a welcome blend of narrative with an underlying conservation message ... the underlying message is excellent — adventure mixed with fact and just thing to hook a youngster into wanting to explore the world."
-- **Descent Magazine**

"*Bumbling Through Borneo* is an adventurous tale of backpacking through Borneo that will have you packing your bags and resigning from work without a second thought."
-- **BC Magazine, Hong Kong**

"Much like what Redmond O'Hanlon's book, *Into the Heart of Borneo*, and others like it did for a score of adventure seekers, Thomas Schmidt's book will tantalize those whom long for adventures in far-away places in Asia. There is much in this book to captivate the reader -- the beautifully drawn illustrations, interesting characters, rich histories, encounters with local peoples and their customs, and tidbits about everything from pirates to indigenous cultures to the orangutan. In today's world of tailored tourism, it is refreshing to see Schmidt travel the way travel ought to be done -- with arms, eyes, and mind wide open."
-- **Robert Lee, Ecologist, UNESCO**

VOLUME 1:

WRITTEN AND ILLUSTRATED BY
TOM SCHMIDT

KAKIBUBU
MEDIA
LIMITED

Hong Kong

This is a work of fiction, based upon a true story. Although the author and publisher have made every effort to ensure the accuracy and completeness of information contained in this book, we assume no responsibility for errors, inaccuracies, omissions, or any inconsistency herein. Any slights of people, places, or organizations are unintentional.

NOTICE TO TRAVELLERS: This book is NOT intended for use as a travel guidebook for planning a trip to Borneo. The story that follows is based on travel to Borneo in the early 1990s; since that time, many places, modes of transportation, and means of access have changed significantly; please refer to the appendix of this book for more detailed information related to current events and travel planning.

BUMBLING THROUGH BORNEO

Published by Kakibubu Media Limited
Hong Kong

www.kakibubu.com

Copyright © 1992, 2009, 2011, 2021 Thomas A. Schmidt

First Printing 1992
Second Printing 2009, revised
Third Printing 2011, revised
2021, revised

All Rights Reserved. This book is protected by copyright. No part of this publication, including interior design, cover design, and icons, may be reproduced, stored in a retrieval system or transmitted in any form or by any means (electronic, mechanical, photocopying, recording or otherwise) -- except by a reviewer who may quote brief passages in a review to be printed in a magazine, newspaper, or on the Web -- without the prior written permission from the Publisher. For information, please contact Kakibubu Media Limited, B1, 24/F, Fortune Factory Bldg, 40 Lee Chung St, Chai Wan, Hong Kong

ISBN 978-988-18066-5-9

Trademarks: "Bumbling Traveller" and the Bumbling Traveller logo are registered trademarks of Kakibubu Media Limited and may not be used without written permission.

ATTENTION CORPORATIONS, UNIVERSITIES, COLLEGES, AND PROFESSIONAL ORGANIZATIONS: Quantity discounts are available on bulk purchases of this book for educational, gift purposes, or as premiums for increasing magazine subscriptions or renewals. Special books or book excerpts can also be created to fit specific needs. For more information, please contact Kakibubu Media Limited.

Cover Design and Bumbling Traveller logo by Pamela J. Trail

Dedicated to backpackers across the world ...

"See the world before you leave it..."
- Unknown

Acknowledgements:

I would like to thank the following individuals who assisted in the production of this publication:

My parents for their unending support; Kate for her love, infinite patience and understanding; Jennifer Sarbiewski for her excellent editorial eye; Pamela Trail for her graphic wizardry and story development, Erica Arakawa who first convinced me to keep a journal of my travels decades ago; Johan and all of the travel companions with whom I've had a multitude of adventures and misadventures over the years; The Borneo Project, Peter Cookson-Smith, John Batten, Norman deBrackinghe, John Hirsch, Lorraine Hahn, Jon Vogels, James and Duncan at May Union Printing and Tom Shanley for all giving me their valuable time and input throughout the whole process -- and of course, the kind hospitable people of Sarawak whom I encountered on my journeys there throughout the years ...

PROLOGUE:

The mysterious nondescript parcel came to Bob out of the blue. His overworked life as an architect in Hong Kong had become increasingly tedious, until that fateful afternoon upon receiving the daily mail. The unmarked packet contained a cryptic handwritten note:

> *Your journey begins now -*
>
> *SARAWAK*
>
> *A great reward awaits you up the Rejang River ...*

Also enclosed in the envelope was an assortment of Hong Kong Dollar bank notes and a one-way plane ticket in his name from Hong Kong to Singapore.

Bob was convinced this was some kind of joke.

However, upon quizzing colleagues, friends and family, no one could offer an explanation. He suffered sleepless nights for a week before his architectural firm downsized. He was left unemployed and burned out; was the world conspiring to get him to travel and take time off?

He knew the Malaysian state of Sarawak was situated on the island of Borneo, but he had never visited there .... for Bob, the word alone evoked exotic imagery of wild, untamed jungle inhabited by tribes of headhunters.

Throwing caution to the wind, he took the plunge and followed his intuition. Temporarily packing up his life in Hong Kong and hastily outfitting himself with a variety of mismatched gear, he set off in search of adventure as well as the identity of who had sent him the mysterious invitation to travel to Borneo!

His journey had indeed begun ...

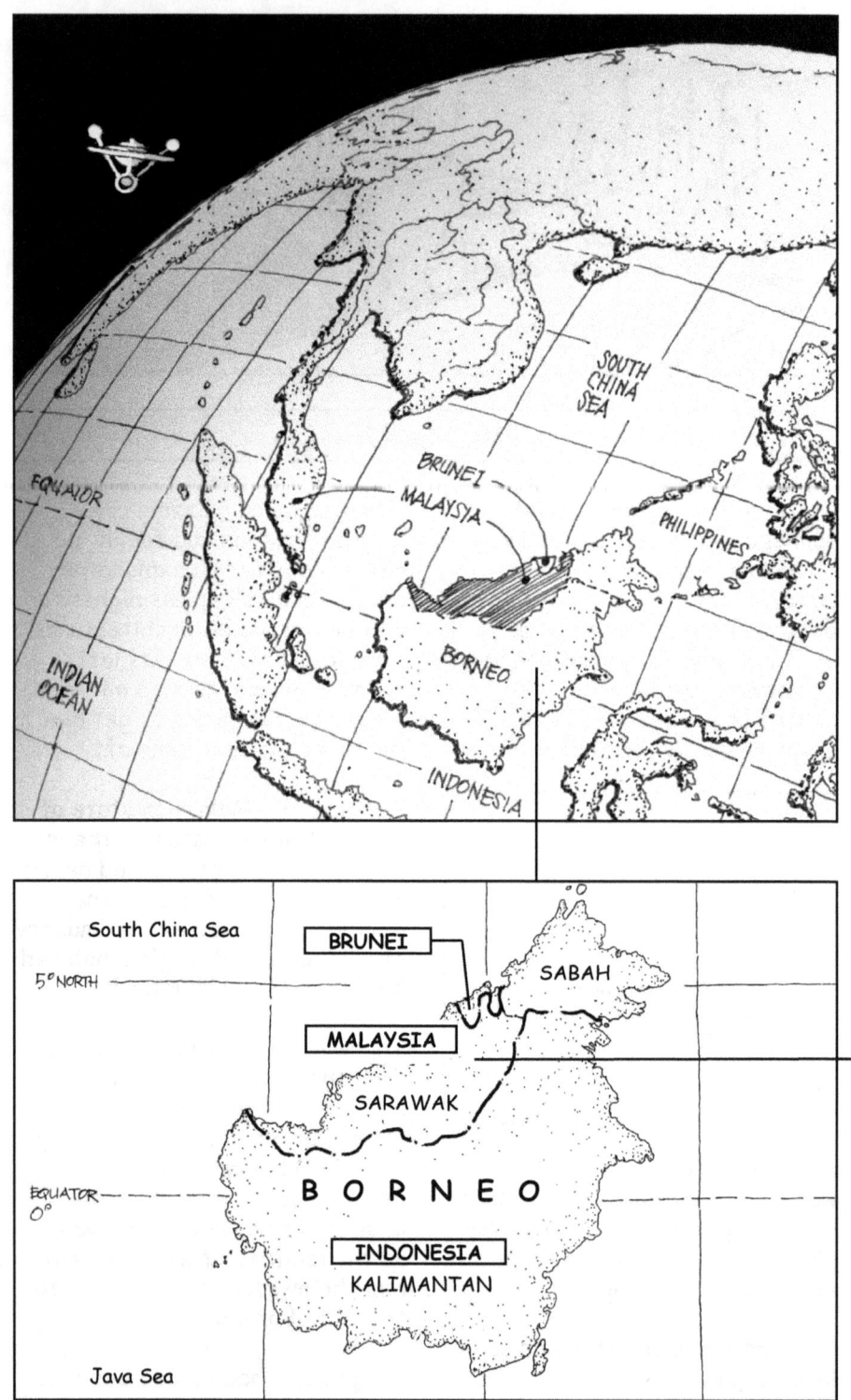

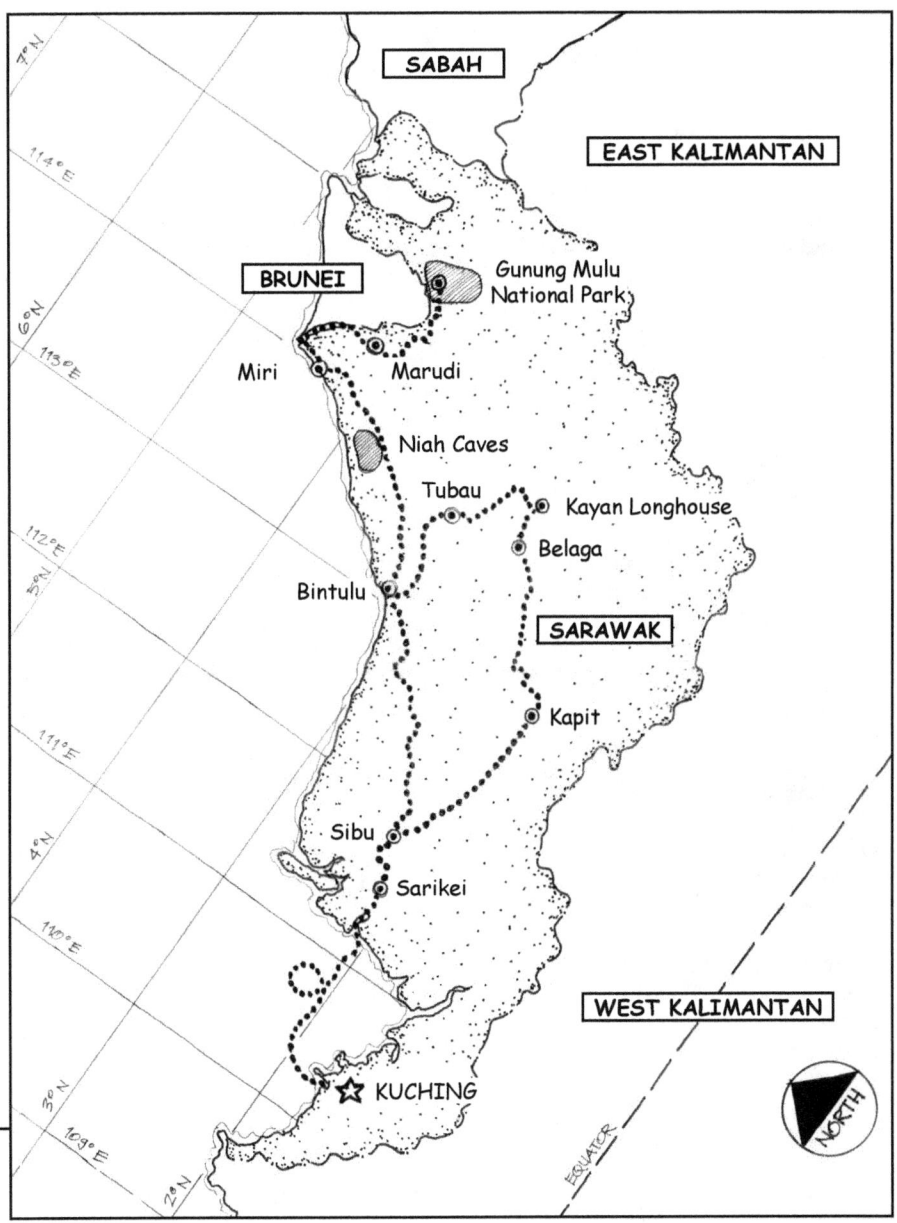

The island of **Borneo** covers an area of about 751,000 sq. km. (290,000 sq. mi.), or slightly larger than the US state of Texas. With a total population of over 16 million, this lushly forested equatorial island is shared by three countries: Malaysia, Indonesia, and Brunei. The Malaysian portion of the island, also referred to as East Malaysia, consists of **Sarawak** (home of the Rejang River), and **Sabah** (containing the island's highest point, Mt. Kinabalu, at 4,100 m. high).

SARAWAK IN A NUTSHELL:

GEOGRAPHY & CLIMATE:

Most of Sarawak's 124,450 sq. km. was once covered by primary rainforest, which is reported to be rapidly disappearing. An alluvial coastal plain is backed by rolling country that is intersected by mountains and innumerable rivers. This equatorial climate is strongly influenced by Northeast monsoons (Nov - May) and Southwest monsoons (Jun - Oct) resulting in temperatures ranging from 25 - 30 degrees C in the lowlands, and 22 - 28 degrees C in the mountainous regions. The mean annual rainfall is relatively high at 2,300 mm, and coupled with a relative humidity of 80%- 85%, provides conditions for a habitat teeming with life.

ECONOMY:

Sarawak's economy is predominantly based in agriculture. With cash crop production (rubber, palm oil, pepper, and sago) concentrated in the coastal zone, the interior relies on subsistence, shifting agriculture, increasingly palm oil, and most notably timber extraction. Although rice is widely grown, palm oil, petroleum products, timber, and rubber continue to be the primary exports. The national currency is the Malaysian Ringgit.

PEOPLE & LANGUAGE:

Of Sarawak's 2.2 million people, Malaysian Chinese constitute roughly 30% of the population while the Ibans (Sea Dayaks) comprise another 30%. The indigenous Malay ethnic group comprises another 20% while many smaller ethnic groups (Kayan, Melinau, Bidayuh, Kenyah, Kelabit, Penan, and Punan) account for the remaining 20% of the population. Despite Malaysia's national language, Bahasa Malaysia (Malay), this multiculturalism has resulted in the retention of a variety of other languages and dialects, including Hokkien, Cantonese, Mandarin and English.

HISTORY:

One of the earliest ruling entities in Sarawak's recent history began with the visit of James Brooke -- an English adventurer and former military officer of the East India Company -- in 1839. After aiding the Sultan of Brunei in suppressing a revolt, he was installed as "Raja" over a certain sector of modern-day Sarawak, where he endeavored to suppress piracy and headhunting. In 1850, Sarawak was recognized as a separate state and continued to grow through annexation and land purchases until 1905. After a lengthy succession of ruling Brookes and the devastating Japanese occupation during World War II, Sarawak ceded to the British Crown in 1946. In 1963, Sarawak joined Malaysia, and is now one of Malaysia's two eastern states.

THE CAST OF CHARACTERS:

BOB

Bumbling American architect on a mysterious quest up the fabled Rejang River in search of an enigmatic "great reward." Recently unemployed, he has a knack for finding trouble in even the most unlikely places ...

JON

Adventurous Swedish carpenter with severe allergies travelling around the world, with a tentative extended stop in Australia. Silent and observant, he is an avid collector of antique tribal masks from across the world ...

UHH ... I ZINK I BROUGHT ZEE WRONG MAP ...

KEN

Intrepid Australian electrician on his way back home "down under" to work in the mines after a year of backpacking through Asia. Always eyeing the women, his prized possession is a weathered Akubra felt hat that rarely leaves his head ...

FRANZ

Zany German artist with a penchant for collecting cooking spices from his travels. Having spent the past two years travelling the world learning new languages, he attempts to traverse Borneo for further island-hopping in Indonesia ...

DAY 1:

It was impossible to sleep on the turbulent flight from Hong Kong to Singapore; a fellow passenger had vomited on my lap, and an annoying child kicked the back of my seat through the duration of the flight. What a great start...

My friends and family were convinced that I had gone absolutely insane -- and for the first time, I was beginning to believe them. Why was an unemployed American architect travelling to the heart of Borneo on a whim?

I was decidedly a bumbling traveller that had absolutely no plan and no real destination in mind. I kept referring to the mysterious note; could it have been some type of code? More importantly, who had sent it to me in the first place?

What or who would be waiting for me far up the Rejang River in the heart of Sarawak? And the "great reward" ... was I an unwitting sucker for some type of contest? The mysterious parcel had contained a small sum of money, so I was determined to make the money last as long as possible.

Upon arrival at Singapore's Changi International Airport, I flipped open my guidebook to the budget accommodation section, and soon headed to Bencoolen Street -- an area reputed to have numerous cheap guesthouses.

Staggering beneath the weight of my enormous backpack, I was spotted by a tout as soon as I had disembarked from the bus. "Hello mister, you need place to stay?"

I agreed to follow the tout through the intense humidity to Lee's Traveller Guesthouse. Situated in a nondescript residential building, this traveller's mecca appeared reasonably clean. I was offered a bed in a dormitory-style room.

After throwing my pack on an empty top bunk, I soon struck up a conversation with a fellow traveller who inhabited the bed below mine. This Swedish backpacker named Jon, had also just arrived in Singapore. He had been travelling overland for months, starting in Sweden, passing through Russia and China, and finally ending up in Singapore.

We hit it off immediately. After listening to his travel tales, I divulged the bizarre set of circumstances that had landed me in Singapore. His jaw dropped when I mentioned that I intended to travel to Sarawak -- he was oddly headed there the following day!

This eerie coincidence actually put me more at ease; perhaps we could travel together as I unravelled this mystery. Jon also seemed excited at the prospect of having a travel partner. I quickly dashed out to a nearby travel agent and procured a last minute flight ticket from nearby Johor Bahru to Kuching -- what luck.

That evening, we continued our conversation at a recommended "steamboat" hot pot restaurant, and exchanged mutual visions of thrashing through uncharted jungle searching for wild tribes of headhunters, as we guzzled a few icy Tiger beers. I had become so totally caught up in the moment, that the uncertainty of why I had decided to travel slowly faded.

DAY 2:

He was carefully scrutinizing the various stamps in my tattered blue passport before he shot a suspecting glance at my unshaven face. This brown uniformed immigration officer rattled off a standard array of questions to discern why this foreigner had come to visit his home: the Malaysian state of Sarawak.

I found it hard to believe that I was actually stepping foot on the renowned island of Borneo. Arriving from Johor Bahru in West Malaysia, I soon found that my new travel companion, Jon, had a great sense of humor in addition to sharing a variety of interests apart from architecture and construction.

The tension finally dissipated as the officer emblazoned a cluttered page of my passport with yet another colorful immigration stamp. A tourist visa for thirty days -- how much ground could we possibly cover in a month?

We had arrived at the provincial capital of Kuching. Cracking open my guidebook, I imagined what adventures might lie in store for us. We were determined to follow the Rejang River into the interior of this ancient island of headhunters -- "great reward" or not -- and to experience the magnificent rainforests of Borneo.

We grabbed a local newspaper to get a sense of local issues and recent news, as some guidebooks are often hopelessly out of date. One recurring theme throughout the newspaper drew our interest: deforestation.

It was apparent that widespread logging and palm oil plantations throughout Sarawak and the neighboring Indonesian Kalimantan provinces were major environmental issues here. It was further believed that the recent lack of precipitation and consequential regional rationing of water in the area could have been attributed to the recent climatic changes during the past few decades.

Were the inexplicable changes in weather patterns, and disruption of delicately balanced ecosystems a result of the island's rapid deforestation to produce exports to timber-hungry nations while filling the coffers of big businesses?

We pondered the ramifications of activities that boost a nation's economy, yet result in adverse environmental changes affecting life on a global scale.

Sadly, the most "developed" countries were probably the biggest culprits around.

My attention soon shifted to an otherworldly article highlighting the orbiting International Space Station high above our planet. I told myself this was a wild time to be alive: Witnessing the decay of our planet while pushing new frontiers! How soon would enterprising people be selling plots of land on the Moon and Mars?

Shifting my mind back to terra firma, we checked into the Kuching Hotel, and wandered around Sarawak's capital city in search of dinner. I continued my discussion with Jon about the deforestation issue. We wondered what the people of Sarawak thought about what was happening in their own backyard. We would find out soon enough.

DAY 3:

After spending the night at the economical Kuching Hotel, the morning began with an informative stop at the Kuching Tourist Information Office. Jon and I grabbed an assortment of maps and leaflets describing Sarawak's extensive cultural heritage, and inquired how we could best proceed up the Rejang River.

As an introduction to this fascinating land, the majority of the day was spent at the Victorian style Sarawak Museum poring over exhibits of wildlife, handicrafts, and ethnographic information relating to this region. Originally built in 1891, the museum also contained an offshore oil drilling exhibit which described the drilling and refining operations of the black gold from which the tiny adjacent Kingdom of Brunei and so many other countries of the world derive their wealth.

My Swedish woodworking companion was immediately drawn to exhibits of various carved wooden masks from Sarawak's past. Elaborately carved masks would be created for certain ceremonies in a village, with their facial characteristics coinciding with the nature of the ceremony. Many were painted with black and white dye to emphasize certain features. Red was often used to impart a demonic presence.

There was also a temporary exhibit on loan featuring a scrap of parchment written in an extinct indecipherable Easter Island language, Rongorongo; noteworthy in that it was discovered in Sarawak, an astounding 15,000 km away from its source.

We departed the highly informative Sarawak Museum and wandered aimlessly along Kuching's relaxed streets.

Jon quizzed several shopkeepers, "So, what does Kuching mean?" Although "Kuching" does translate into "cat" in Malay, one shopkeeper contended it was a variation of the Indian name for "port" ("Cochin"), as Kuching was first settled by Indian traders who set up their operations at Santubong.

We strolled along the waterfront in the late afternoon and returned to the tourist information office before closing. A very helpful woman informed us of a variety of options to begin our journey up the Rejang River, ranging from travelling as semi-stowaways on a cargo ship, to prohibitively expensive customized package tours.

At an outdoor restaurant, Jon and I discussed our options as we savored several small skewered bits of chicken with a delectable peanut sauce. This tasty chicken satay was followed by a spicy coconut prawn paste-based soup served with rice vermicelli, eggs, prawns, chicken, and deep fried tofu -- known as "Sarawak Laksa."

We were relieved that we had entered a land with delicious local food.

Suitably impressed with this multi-cultural city, we retired early that evening and planned the days ahead -- we had only a month to spend in Sarawak.

With aspirations of staying in the longhouses of these forest-dwelling people, we agreed to commence our journey up the Rejang River the following day.

DAY 4:

"I've always wanted to stowaway on a cargo ship!" exclaimed Jon. The tourist office had informed us that the most economical way from Kuching to Sibu was via a twice-weekly cargo ship. Our money was scarce; this sounded like the perfect option.

After a quick dash to the market and haggling to purchase eight liters of mineral water and an assortment of fruit, we stumbled through the afternoon heat to the Kuching shipyard. We arrived well before the projected departure time to find a rusting cargo ship, groaning under its own weight.

Delving into the frenzy of activity, we ducked between workers hoisting bags of rice and wooden crates stuffed full of chirping young chicks, and proceeded up a precariously narrow gangplank toward a small oval-shaped doorway. As we boarded, the bottom of one my food bags gave way, sending several bottles of drinking water plunging into the water far below.

Jon rolled his eyes with disgust, as we made our way to a raised platform in a section of the cargo hold containing a variety of potted plants and several thousand cases of chicken eggs. Hoisting our backpacks onto an elevated sleeping platform, we were greeted by two chatty elderly Malay women who also appeared to be passengers. They didn't seem to mind that we couldn't understand a word they were telling us in Bahasa Malaysia. My motto: when in doubt, smile, nod and be polite.

 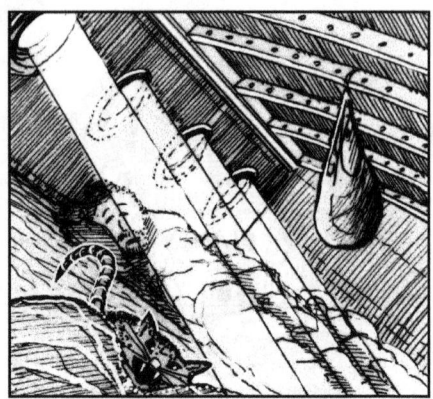

Piecing together the fragments of Malay we did understand, we eventually ascertained that one woman was 73 years old and had six children. More families began appearing carrying gargantuan bags of foodstuffs and clothing. One Malay woman began cackling while tugging Jon's blonde beard, as he gently recoiled. "This happened to me in China as well," he complained.

A few other budget travellers had also staked out places to sleep on the boat. We were soon approached by a cheerful Australian named Ken on his way back "down under" to Mt. Isa, Australia, to work as an electrician in the mines there. He taught us an addictive card game that continued well into the night as we slowly floated out of Kuching. During my extended losing streak, Ken chided, "Bob, mate, if we were back in Oz, you'd be drinkin' by now!"

The lightning of an impending storm illuminated paper mills and other riverside industry beneath an ominous night sky. Other boats passed silently in the night as strange lighted buoys swayed in our wake. The zillions of chirping chicks drowned out the old women next to us, as they gossiped and giggled into the night.

It soon began to rain as we pulled the portholes closed. Jolts of lightning cast a momentary spotlight through the circular apertures, illuminating the resident rats of this vessel that were quickly closing in. Scaling vertical surfaces effortlessly, the rats soon scattered after water began to leak onto our sleeping surface from the roof above. It was then the captain hobbled past and informed us that the 18-hour journey would be closer to 30 hours. Ken muttered, "I sure could use a beer 'bout now."

Reality began to set in. What in the world was I doing on a decrepit rat-ridden cargo ship? Had I completely lost my mind to leave the comfort and modernity of Hong Kong to suffer like this? We had barely enough food and water to survive. What was I in search of anyway? I unfolded the mysterious note once again, hoping to glean some kind of clue. A "great reward" awaits me at the top of the Rejang River? The cargo ship heaved on ...

THE SIBU CARGO EXPRESS:

- Stoic Captain up top in the bridge -- steering vessel with authentic helplessly spinning Gilligan's Island steering wheel ...

- First Mate: Liter bottles of Anker Beer ...

- Large steel crane used for hoisting cargo into main hold -- doubles as lightning rod in stormy weather ...

- Unidentifiable mystery cargo with corresponding mystery odors ...

- Jovial, rambunctious crew loading cargo day and night on upper and lower decks ...

- Bags of food suspended from roof (clever anti-rat food protection tactic) ...

- Mutant cargo ship rodents with uncanny ability to scale vertical surfaces in total darkness ...

- Weary travellers attempting to sleep beneath semi-dry portions of a leaky ceiling ...

- Local Sarawak residents snoozing peacefully among a forest of potted plants below a raised platform ...

- Zillions of fragile eggs on a violently rocking ship ...

- The ominous all-too-scary smelling hole-in-the-floor toilet!

- Hundreds of wooden cases crammed full of wildly chirping chicks ...

THE REJANG RIVER:

As one of the "great rivers" of Borneo, the **Rejang River** ("Batang Rejang") flows approximately 560 km. (350 mi.) from the island's hinterland to the South China Sea, making it the longest river in Malaysia. The upper part of the Rejang River, the Balui River, is home to Malaysia's largest hydroelectric project, the Bakun Hydroelectric Dam (see facing page).

In addition to acting as a drainage system for a vast rainforest catchment area, the mighty Rejang River and its many tributaries is the lifeline for the thousands of small indigenous communities located along its banks. Serving as the primary artery of transportation to the many longhouses through a network of express boats, the Rejang also provides an important source of sustenance to the various communities and wildlife along its length.

Located 60 km. upriver from the mouth of the Rejang, Sibu is the river's largest town and commercial gateway for oceangoing vessels. While the Iban largely populate the lower regions of the river, the smaller towns of Kanowit, Kapit, and Belaga further upriver, are home to many smaller ethnic groups including the Kayan, Kenyah, and the once nomadic Penan.

The past four decades have witnessed significant changes to the once crystal clear Rejang River. Increases in silting and the resulting decreases in river depths have been attributed to erosion and deforestation due to logging, new palm oil plantations, sand extraction, as well as other development activities, including the construction of the Bakun Dam. These fundamental changes to the Rejang River are also said to be a contributing factor in the increased frequency of flooding of riverside towns. It was widely reported that indicators of the deteriorating water quality -- especially along urbanized stretches of the river -- include decreases in oxygen levels, and increases in organic pollutants and water-borne disease, adversely affecting aquatic life. This has often been exacerbated by the discharge of sewage and wastewater directly into the river from the presence of squatters whom are not provided with proper sewerage and rubbish disposal facilities.

THE BAKUN HYDROELECTRIC DAM:

Situated 37 km. upstream from Belaga upon on the Balui River -- a tributary and main source of the Rejang River -- the **Bakun Hydroelectric Dam** is one of Malaysia's most ambitious, yet controversial infrastructure projects.

Fully commissioned in 2014, the Bakun Hydroelectric Dam is one of the largest and tallest dams in Asia. Mired in controversy for almost five decades, the 207-meter high dam has a reservoir with a surface area of almost 70,000 hectares – equivalent to the size of Singapore. Conceived in the 1970s and finally beginning construction in 2002, this massive project was undertaken by a Malaysia-China joint venture employing a workforce of thousands, in addition to a variety of engineers, consultants, and specialists. Conceived as a long-term solution for Peninsular and East Malaysia's growing demand for electricity, it had been proposed that surplus power might also feed into a trans-Borneo power grid to supply electricity throughout the Malaysian states of Sarawak and Sabah as well as Brunei and Indonesia's Kalimantan provinces. In addition to the creation of jobs related to its construction, this project is capable of producing 2,400 megawatts (MW) of clean, emission-free electricity.

However, it appears this solution for clean power came at a price. Long opposed by the affected Dayak communities, followed by a number of non-governmental organizations (NGO's) and environmental groups -- citing extensive environmental damage -- this project has reportedly resulted in the destruction of vast areas of rainforest to accommodate the project's required reservoir and catchment areas. The reported deterioration of water quality, and increased silting of areas downriver has been a constant point of controversy. In addition to the displacement of over 100 protected terrestrial species from their natural habitat, almost 10,000 Kayan and Kenyah native inhabitants were displaced from their ancestral homes and relocated to Sungai Asap in Bakun. The relocation of these subsistence farmers, who traditionally relied on the forest for food and shelter, to resettlement villages resulted in a number of socio-economic problems.

THE CHINESE OF SIBU:

INTRODUCTION:

Sibu is the second largest town in Sarawak and serves as the main trading center between the coast and the vast hinterland along the Rejang river area. It was originally named "New Foochow" after the Hokkien and Teochew (Chaozhou) Chinese immigrants from the Fujian province of China. Today, roughly 60% of Sibu's population is Chinese.

HISTORY:

The Chinese have had a presence in Sibu since the mid-1800s, the majority of whom were Hokkien traders from Fujian. As traders, and as one of the most affluent groups, they established the earliest financial institutions in the area. At that time, there was also a smaller Cantonese population involved in small scale logging of the copious reserves of durable "ironwood" trees, which were exported to Hong Kong.

With plans of creating a prosperous community similar to the Dutch outpost of Java in Indonesia, James Brooke -- Sarawak's first "White Raja" -- hoped to rule over and expand this early outpost through the introduction of Chinese settlers. While the existing Cantonese and Hokkien traders were primarily interested in commerce, they were not as interested in long-term settlement. Therefore in 1880, to attract large-scale settlement, Brooke offered Chinese companies free agricultural land, temporary housing and other incentives to attract potential groups of Chinese migrants.

However, there was not substantial interest until almost twenty years later when he sought the assistance of Wong Nai Siong -- an exiled Chinese scholar and Christian convert who lived in Sibu to avoid religious persecution in his homeland. At Brooke's request, Wong returned to China to recruit his fellow countrymen to emigrate to a "new life" in Sarawak. As a reward for the successful large-scale Chinese migration that soon followed, Wong was appointed as "port master" of Sibu.

Unfortunately, early Chinese settlers suffered widespread deaths from malaria, and their unfamiliarity with local agricultural practices resulted in failed crops. Brooke's plan for creating income from levied taxes on a successful agricultural industry never came to fruition. Wong found himself in a difficult position, and due to the resulting opium trade and gambling activities that had proliferated, he soon became alienated and returned to China. The Chinese migrant farmers and fishermen who remained in Sibu settled to become laborers and blacksmiths. As timber became an increasingly valuable product, many entrepreneurial Chinese started timber companies as the port continued to flourish. Today, many historical Chinese buildings remain throughout Sibu, and Chinese continue to dominate the economic sector of Sarawak.

DAY 5:

I regained consciousness early the next morning to the sound of shouting crew members. The sky was bright and the cargo was in the process of being unloaded at this port of Sarikei. The Malay women had disembarked along with their innumerable bags. I had discovered that rats had gnawed through my backpack while we slept, leaving a gaping hole.

Since we had a few hours in port before departing, we disembarked and shuffled into the nearest restaurant we could find. A few Ringgit bought a delicious plate of "Mee Goreng" (fried noodles) and "Kopi Susu" (coffee with sweetened condensed milk). After departing at noon, I spent the voyage to Sibu sewing up the ragged hole in my backpack with a needle and a long strand of waxed dental floss.

Our 25-hour sojourn, spanning two days, ended in Sibu just before sundown. We learned that this gateway to the mighty Rejang River was the second largest town in Sarawak. Now boasting a predominantly Chinese population of around 250,000, it was said the enterprising Chinese settlers from generations ago, now dominate the economy.

After disembarking and stumbling out into the blinding late afternoon sunlight, we attempted to make some sense of the rudimentary maps in our guidebooks. Ken suggested, "Well mates, I reckon we should find someplace to sleep, and then get a few beers -- I'm parched!" Jon silently nodded in agreement.

We rambled into town and discovered a tiny guesthouse in a dismal-looking back alley. After a claustrophobic voyage, Ken had unofficially joined Jon and me as travel companions. He was, after all, heading in the same direction.

We found a shared room in a guesthouse that appeared relatively clean, and began the brief negotiation process with the owner.

Sibu was the launching point for a trip further upriver, but how would we actually proceed? Upon quizzing the guesthouse owner, a hard-bargaining Chinese man, he kindly provided a schedule of regularly departing boats up to Kapit -- the next major town upriver.

After thanking him for his assistance, we explored the crowded "pasar malam" (night market). Browsing through its hundreds of market stalls, we indulged in all types of culinary oddities and delicacies.

A chatty stall owner chanted, "Hello! Pepper! Pepper!" As he vigorously promoted Sarawak black pepper, we wondered if he had consumed a bit too much himself. He contended that Malaysia ranked within the top five pepper producing nations, and that Sarawak pepper was exported to more than 40 countries. He went on to explain the various types of black, green and white peppers -- as well as various pepper products. Jon took a whiff and began sneezing uncontrollably.

We retreated from this evening of culinary education to our guesthouse for a much needed night's sleep on an actual mattress -- one of those simple luxuries that is not appreciated until one goes without.

DAY 6:

Despite a restless night of sleep enduring endless snores and Jon's constant sneezing, we began a hopeful journey to Kapit, the first major checkpoint for travel farther upriver. Filling our stomachs with several "roti canai" (a doughy pancake-like flatbread) for breakfast, we climbed aboard a narrow steel-hulled boat powered by twin diesel engines.

Our express boat, resembling a salvaged fuselage of a jet airplane with the wings removed, was aerodynamically designed for blasting up the river. We sped up the mighty highway of water, the Rejang River, perched atop the luggage rack beneath a scorching midday sun. Jon photographed huge timber barges slowly floating downriver, and chugging tugboats towing an entangled mess of ancient tree trunks.

My gaze shifted to the occasional Iban "longhouse" along the river's edge. This linear series of local dwellings, specific to the island of Borneo, floated above ground on a system of posts and was covered by one large communal roof.

We received stares and waves from residents tiptoeing down a system of gangplanks to bathe in the muddy river below. Small children bobbed beneath the shade of wooden docks to seek refuge from a harsh tropical sun.

I was secretly excited to finally be travelling up the great river described on my cryptic note. But what did it all mean?

I spent most of the three-hour journey to Kapit chatting with a Malaysian hydrologist who fretted about the unusual dryness of the season, as well as the decreasing clarity and low levels of this life-sustaining river.

Disembarking at the sprawling riverside town of Kapit, our group's mission to seek accommodation was soon accomplished upon asking a nearby cafe owner. A small room above his cafe was affordable, if split among the three of us. Haggling the price a bit, we finally struck a deal.

While trying to determine the process of proceeding farther upriver, we received a different response from everyone with whom we spoke. We relayed our experience to the friendly cafe owner, who quickly escorted us to the nearby police station to obtain a permit for further travel.

At last; it seemed as if we were making progress.

Procuring a permit consisted of chatting with six yawning policemen while duly entering our names, passport numbers, and occupations into a dusty ledger. The massive book was returned to its place beneath a heap of crumpled papers that would probably not be moved for the next decade.

Over a plate of noodles, Jon, Ken and I discussed the next stretch of the journey. Our next stop would be a town named Belaga.

We learned from two backpackers arriving from destinations upstream, that in the past week alone, a perilous set of rapids upriver had claimed three lives, destroyed two boats, and left one traumatized traveller stranded overnight on a huge rock in the middle of the river.

DAY 7:

After the previous day's tale of the killer rapids, I was slightly relieved to discover there were no regular boats headed upriver today. Owing to a lack of rainfall, the rapids upstream were too shallow and unnavigable; we had to wait at least another day or two.

Someone had suggested a visit to a nearby swimming hole to "beat the heat." We went about hiring a minivan for the day, and were joined by a Scottish medical student living in Kapit whom we had met the evening before, in addition to a silent, antisocial dark-haired Portuguese woman.

After haggling with the driver for a daily price, we sped down the road out of town as an ethereal song by a band called Jetopa filled the van. Jon continued sneezing.

We sailed through overgrown jungle and stopped at a trail head. We anxiously clambered down slippery moss-covered rocks and tromped through several rivers until we came upon the scintillating pond. Set below a picturesque waterfall, the pond was filled with ...

... bathing, frolicking Italians!

One man, clad in an impossibly tiny nylon swimsuit, puffed on a cigarette and pounded a portable cassette player, wondering why his tiny machine refused to function in this humid tropical jungle. We joined the jovial Italians in this refreshingly cool water. Their laughter permeated the surrounding jungle as we took turns diving into this murky pool shaded by lush canopy trees towering high overhead.

Jon muttered, "Uh oh!" as the sky began to rumble and the sun disappeared. We raced back to the trail head at the first hint of rain. We were warned that flash floods were always a possibility.

A group of us huddled beneath a leaky Nepalese paper umbrella that Jon withdrew from his daypack. In the thirty minutes we had waited for the minivan to return, the umbrella had turned to pulp and everyone was thoroughly soaked from the endless cascade of rain that splashed down upon us from the broad palm leaves overhead.

Our small adventure ended on an irate note when our driver had cleverly added an extra zero to the price of the van upon our return to Kapit. Wringing out our drenched shirts, we insisted on paying him his original quote, and defiantly marched away.

Several of us later regrouped for a tasty meal of sweet and sour pork and fresh vegetables at a small cafe. Ken exclaimed, "I don't believe it. They have Guinness here!" As we ordered several pints of the surprisingly available Guinness Stout, several elderly Chinese diners joined our table of interlopers, one by one, and praised the medicinal properties of this murky Irish beverage. They were soon buying us round after round.

The Guinness kept flowing as we discussed topics ranging from international politics to Sarawak's many environmental issues until all hours of the night. It was an excellent chance for our Chinese friends to practice English, while we learned a bit more Malay. The beers counteracted Jon's distracting sneezes and allowed a decent night of sleep.

DAY 8:

The day began with an annoying electronic beep from Ken's cheap digital wristwatch. Jon and I arose at 6:00 a.m. and blindly scrambled down to the Kapit jetty to check whether any boats were headed upstream. Ken remained comatose from one too many beers.

The heavy rains from the previous day proved to be a blessing in disguise. There were express boats running that morning through the often impassible "Pelagus Rapids" to Belaga.

Ken's head was pounding as we climbed into another tubular, streamlined express boat. We escaped the chilly air conditioned interior and screeching Kung Fu videos by taking a rooftop seat on the luggage rack in the cool misty morning air.

We began our journey upriver. A lone logger passed us silently in the opposite direction, balancing on a single log amidst a floating forest of felled timber. The riverbanks and hills above gradually emerged from the mist revealing lumber camps as well as various Iban longhouses covered with corrugated metal roofing.

The boat periodically swooped toward the river's edge as a waiting family raced alongside and leapt up on board while catapulting live chickens, sacks of rice, and hunting rifles onto the deck. The captain, wedged into the nose of this vessel, zigzagged across the width of the river in a trance-like state. He alone knew the deepest parts of the river to keep us from running aground.

Preparing for the worst, the crew had ushered us inside when we had reached the infamous Pelagus Rapids, which had claimed more than a dozen lives in the past month. Small swirling whirlpools began to form, undoubtedly covering a treacherous array of boat-destroying rock formations below.

With precise maneuvering, our ascent past jagged rocks skewering teetering remnants of ill-fated boats went surprisingly smoothly. We passed more longhouses -- much older than many of the ones we had seen downriver. Residents casually bathed and washed dishes in the river. Groups of small children periodically popped out from behind trees and began shouting and waving wildly. A reciprocal wave triggered ecstatic laughter.

We finally reached Belaga after five long hours.

The three members of our small group disembarked along with a handful of other travellers as we scaled our way up a gangplank to the main town.

The stilted town of Belaga revealed seemingly random structures placed at impossible angles, all connected by a series of boardwalks. We passed a group of old tattooed women sitting on their haunches grinning with the telltale red-stained lips that indicated a passion for mildly narcotic Betel nuts. Their earlobes were pierced and elongated -- big loops of skin that had been stretched and weighted down over the years.

Our first piece of business here took place at the Belaga Police Department. Soon, we were granted a permit to proceed farther up the Balie River, a tributary of the Rejang, and to trek overland to Tubau and Bintulu.

 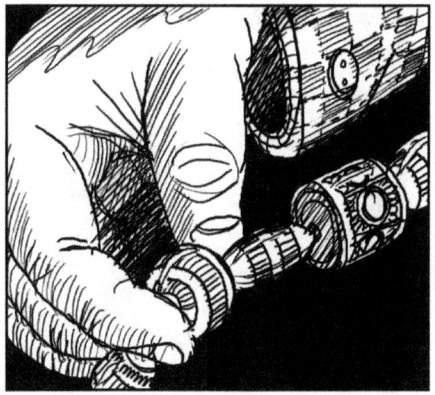

Before embarking on a quest for a place to sleep, Ken soon discovered his guidebook had been swept off the roof of the boat at some point during our journey. He was livid.

After choosing one of the tidier guesthouses on offer in Belaga, we collectively discussed the possibility of trekking to some of the nearby longhouses the following day. Ken concluded, "Well, we definitely need a guide from here on out." Where would we find a guide?

Fortuitously, that evening while dining at a communal table in a nearby restaurant, things began to fall into place. A chatty diner at our table, a Malaysian census officer, casually informed us of his journey farther upriver to his family longhouse. He graciously invited us along -- but only if we were interested.

We were ecstatic to have stumbled upon this great opportunity -- what could be better than being invited to a local's home? Was this the "great reward" I had been promised?

This seemingly westernized Kayan native named Jim still retained his tribal beads around his neck. He explained that beads were originally principal forms of currency before evolving into symbols of social status. In times past, certain beads were worn only at select ceremonies, including births and deaths, or while engaged in battle. He professed that the Kayan place more value on the more intricate and decorative beads. Other tribes held that beads that were colored a deep blue would strengthen an infant's soul, and were draped around the necks of children at such a vulnerable age.

After arranging the logistics with Jim for our boat trip the following day, he naturally asked us to share the cost of petrol and other expenses. We arrived at an equitable agreement, and the three of us headed back to our guesthouse relatively early to rest for tomorrow's adventure.

Upon entering our room, we encountered one of many mutant prehistoric creepy-crawlies that inhabit these parts: a huge housefly-like insect the size of a small bird.

This nightmarish creature was trapped in our room, buzzing around and bashing itself against the lone fluorescent light illuminating our room.

While we decided how to extricate this creature, the bug's trajectory followed an unplanned course into the spinning blades of our ceiling fan. This consequently scored a grand slam, sending the alien insect catapulting across the room directly into Ken's face! Spitting violently and convulsing with disgust, Ken's trauma eventually subsided. We scooped up the quivering carcass with a scrap of paper and flicked it out the window.

Jon cracked open his guidebook and reported that the Sarawak rainforest was home to an incredible variety of more than 8,000 species of flora and more than 20,000 fauna, the majority of which are insects. Our close encounter really wasn't so surprising. The three of us quickly unravelled our tangled mosquito nets and strung them up from various points in the room. Ken was the first inside his net. It was comforting to know that we also had a built-in rotary pest remover whirring overhead, as we drifted off to sleep.

DAY 9:

We met our new friend Jim at the prearranged time of 10:00 a.m. We each paid a small sum to the boatman and climbed aboard a blue longboat loaded down with 40 liters of petrol, various supplies, our backpacks, a local family, and whatever else could be squeezed in.

I wrapped my sarong around my head and shoulders for some protection from the glaring late morning sun. We began gliding upstream upon serene waters toward the source of this once turbulent river.

I was sandwiched next to a woman and her small child who was nestled in a "kelabit" on her back. The intricate beadwork of this baby pouch included shells and animal teeth that produced a gentle rattling sound that reputedly frightened evil spirits away from an infant during the first few months of life.

The chief of the longhouse we were to visit was perched on the bow of the carefully balanced boat. As he gazed into the water ahead, he shouted navigational instructions in tandem with secret hand signals to the motor man at the rear.

A local passenger wedged directly behind me lit up a smoldering conical-shaped cigarette, and carelessly flicked his ashes upon the plastic jugs of petrol that were already quite warm in the tropical sun. Jon and I exchanged nervous glances as we wondered if our boat was a time bomb waiting to go off.

THE SARAWAK LONGBOAT:

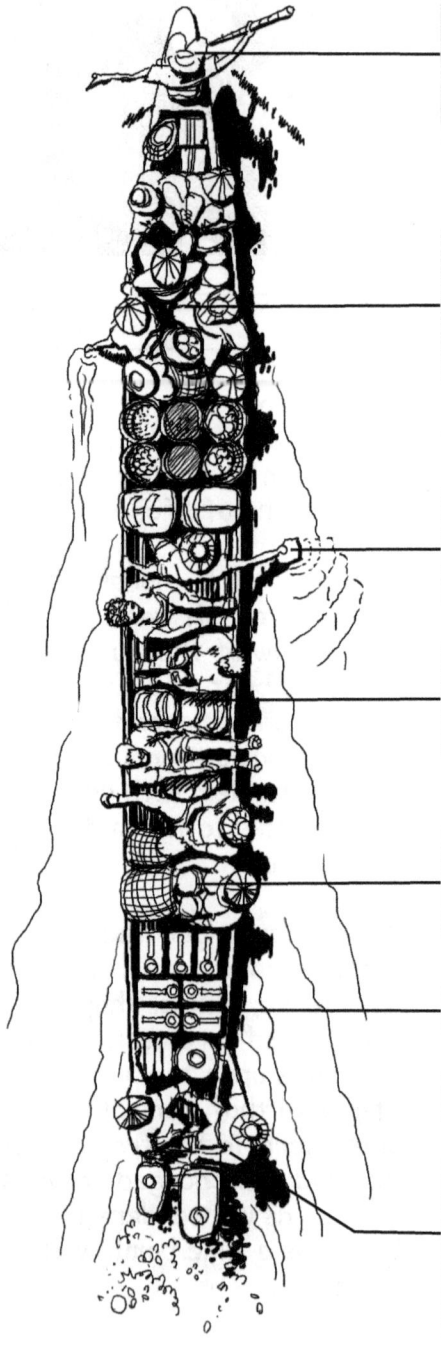

- Longhouse Chief with river-depth measuring stick waving hand signals to boat owner at the rear

- Several local families in transit to their longhouse with innumerable baskets of food and supplies

- Bilge Pump Man -- perpetually scooping water from boat bottom with plastic scoop

- Intrepid travellers with huge backpacks baking under a harsh tropical sun

- Chain-smoking chicken farmer flicking cigarette ashes on extra tanks of warm petrol

- Extra tanks of petrol

- Life Jackets ... in Borneo?

- Two motor men manning dual outboard engines (one primary 40 hp engine, and one smaller engine for shallow water / backup)

Soon after the family in our boat had disembarked, we proceeded farther upstream until we had reached a set of rapids. Jim instructed us to disembark and hike along the riverbank, while the Chief and the boatman gunned the boat's engine and bashed their way up the shallow rapids in a lighter boat.

Climbing along a well trodden path through the dense jungle, we came across a most unexpected sight: a small sacred hut (Salong) perched atop a high intricately carved pole (Kelirieng). We were told this was an elevated mausoleum containing the bones of an old aristocratic family. We studied this curiosity before rejoining the boat after it was maneuvered above the rapids. We were surprised to learn that with each rain-free day, the rapids that we had bypassed were becoming more and more dangerous from an unusually low water level. Our momentum slowed as the Chief reached over the side of the boat and pulled up a fish net at the junction of a tributary just below their longhouse. An old frail man and young girl silently drifted by in a tiny dugout canoe and stared in wonder at our unshaven faces.

The Chief plucked a few river fish from the net and shook his head in frustration. We were told the nearby dam project upstream had adversely affected his catch.

We had finally arrived. Hoisting our unnecessarily heavy packs out of the boat, we scaled a notched log up to a sprawling Kayan longhouse. I made mental notes about the construction, while I gazed in awe of this communal structure that was completely built using materials from the surrounding rainforest.

Jim explained that visitors normally needed to shout for permission to enter a longhouse, but we were trailing the Chief who had bounded up just minutes earlier. After removing our footwear, we climbed up onto a wide verandah that ran the entire length of the longhouse.

A group of young children froze and cast nervous stares as we drifted down the length of the communal verandah of this 75-door house (one door per household).

"Where is everyone?" I inquired. Jim responded that many families were away at small remote dwellings harvesting rice and other crops during harvest time. The majority of the young men of the longhouse had embarked on migratory journeys to seek higher paying jobs as laborers on oil rigs and in lumber camps throughout the state.

We strolled past an elderly man who was hunched over and squatting near the railing on the verandah. His bony outstretched arm prodded interloping chickens that would periodically prance over to steal a few grains of rice that were drying on bamboo mats in the sunshine.

His forearms and feet were covered with greenish-black tattoos that commemorated his past journeys and experiences -- a kind of permanent diary. His mouth contained the red mush of a Betel nut wrapped in a leaf, which he systematically crushed with glittering copper colored metallic teeth.

Like many elders there, his droopy pierced earlobes were almost shoulder length. For women, it was said that the longer the earlobes, the more attractive.

The first stop in our procession along the verandah was a visit to the Chief's "door" (apartment). Proving to be a bit of an entrepreneur, the Chief insisted that we each purchase a beverage from his well-stocked refrigerator.

Refrigerator?!?!

This wasn't such a primitive settlement after all! Even deep in the interior of Borneo, there was no escape from the instantly recognizable American carbonated beverage that "adds life."

After guzzling an obligatory Coke, we returned to an unmarked door behind which contained a segment of the longhouse belonging to Jim's family. We were offered a meal of deer meat and rice topped with a spicy chili sauce before descending to the river with my fellow travellers for an afternoon bath.

Clad in only a sarong, I cautiously entered the river and, following local practice, attempted to wash myself without actually removing the sarong.

I later spent a couple of hours drifting along the length of the verandah observing a few elders busily creating various handicrafts. One man was painting a carved shield, while a nearby woman was weaving a hat from palm fronds. Another woman was weaving a rattan basket hanging from a bamboo rafter above.

This predominantly agricultural society appeared to create various baskets and mats for transporting their crops to and from the longhouse. Each decorative pattern was specifically fashioned according to its function. Different baskets would be created for religious ceremonies than for agricultural purposes.

As we retreated to Jim's "door," the setting sun cast a golden orange beam of light on a lone elderly woman sitting on the floor of an adjacent room to which we were led.

She was momentarily too engaged in her beadwork to look up. Jim mumbled something to her in Kayan which sent the woman into another room. We were seated on rattan mats covering the floor, as the woman returned with a bottle of "Borak" (or "Tuak"), a milky white local rice wine.

Jim explained that visitors arriving at a longhouse were typically offered a welcoming drink of Borak, and unless prohibited by one's religion, refusal of consumption could be considered offensive to the hosts. Ken murmured, "Hmm, don't mind if I do..." as he slurped down the first cup in one swift motion. Jon and I then took the plunge.

By our third bottle of this surprisingly smooth concoction, an old woman residing in the longhouse had lit a brass oil lamp. Soon the chiseled facial features of our hosts took on a surreal quality in the flickering lamp light, not unlike the masks we had seen at the Sarawak Museum.

As we sat in this room devoid of furnishings, another woman joined our circle and began gossiping with the first woman while they simultaneously prepared doses of betel nut with robotic motions.

As they smacked away with their metallic teeth, Jim began to convey to us the inner workings of the longhouse. He explained that major ceremonies were performed collectively by all members of the longhouse; this also helped to minimize internal dissension within the community. When family conflicts arose, the

 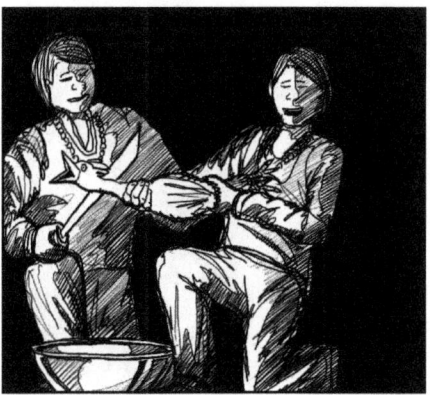

Chief would act as a mediator until a situation was resolved to everyone's satisfaction. I secretly wished people would use this method of conflict resolution in my own litigious society.

We began to consume a fourth bottle when several of Jim's relatives gradually began to return to the longhouse one by one. They had returned from a day out hunting, attending school, or harvesting.

A rotund young woman appeared with a live chicken dangling from a string that bound its feet together. Jim announced that this feathery creature was to be our late night snack.

Visions of pagan rituals and bygone days of headhunting danced through my head as Jim grabbed the chicken's head while his younger brother gripped its legs and wings. A small monkey chained to a post near the kitchen cooking fire was now nervously screeching as the rotund woman lit a fire beneath a cauldron of water.

Ken's diabolical game of cards that had kept us occupied and acted as a good catalyst for inter-cultural communication soon lost its meaning as Jim's machete gently sliced the throat of the creature that may have served as someone's alarm clock earlier that same morning.

Violent spasms swept through the feathery mass that slowly trickled its life away into a stainless steel bowl below. The chicken was soon thrown into the bubbling cauldron of boiling water, plucked of its feathers, and disappeared into the kitchen area to be gutted and cooked. Jon was nauseous and began sneezing uncontrollably once again.

Fortunately, the alcohol from the Borak had numbed the sickening sensation that had gradually crept up inside me. I was never keen on seeing animals slaughtered. But this was life. We were soon served the product of this spectacle over steamed white rice.

There were deadly angled chunks of bone with slight traces of meat; I wondered if the more prized pieces of meat were saved for another meal. We never solved that mystery before the conversation turned from chicken bones to human bones.

Jon dashed to the toilet as Ken and I began to squirm. Although no longer practiced, as far as we knew, the few family heirloom cobweb enshrouded skulls that dangled from the rafters above spurred on a discussion of headhunting.

In Sarawak, headhunting was at one point an integral part of village life. Jim went on to explain that in old times, a man was only considered worthy once he had brought home a head. Only then could he have his palms tattooed, take a wife, and be consulted about important village matters. What a rite of passage.

As he unravelled some tall tales about past headhunting adventures, Jim uncorked yet another bottle of Borak, and went on to explain the significance of tattoos in his culture which were also associated with headhunting. I reflected on the elderly man we had met upon entering the longhouse, and his extensively tattooed body.

As more residents joined our group, the night raged on to a blurry memory of dancing, laughing, drinking more Borak, and hearing tales of the past.

HEADHUNTING IN BORNEO

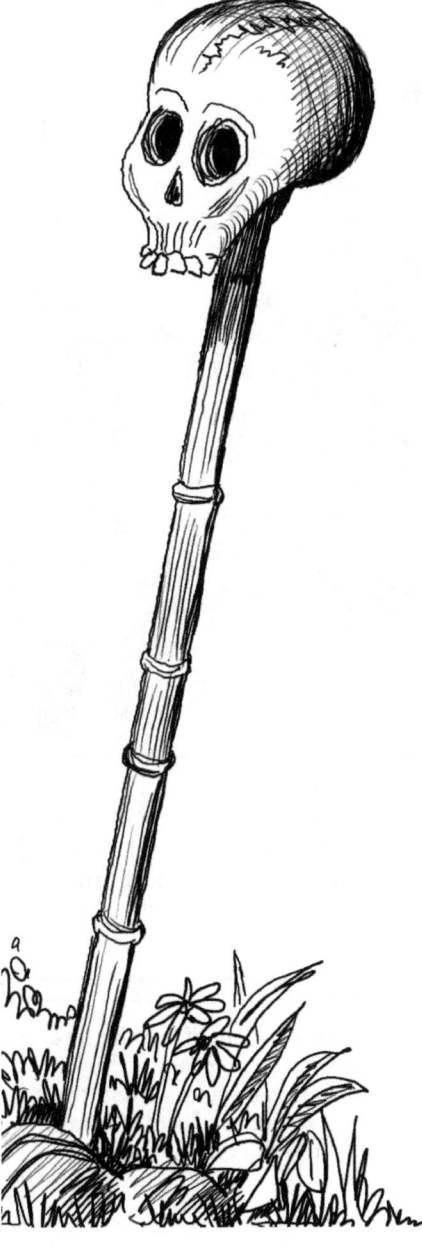

The ancient practice of headhunting among select warring tribes in Borneo ceased over a century ago. In most cases, headhunting was a means of activating a relationship with the spiritual world in order to derive benefit for one's community.

In addition to the spiritual power and vitality that could be replenished or accumulated by capturing an enemy's head (by transferring the vital soul-life of one community to another), there may have been a variety of other reasons the tribes of Borneo embarked on headhunting expeditions. In some tribes, it was said that the magical powers of the heads would bring strength, virtue, and prosperity to the longhouse. Some tribes used headhunting as a method of territorial control and expansion relative to their forest resources. Among some groups, headhunting was a ritual activity rather than an act of war, instigated to terminate a period of collective mourning for a dead member of the community, or to insure a bountiful rice harvest (some tribes held that rice possessed a soul that required placation).

The taking of heads was often regarded as a sign of male prowess, prestige, as well as an indicator of a worthy marriage partner. A successful headhunting expedition would be welcomed home by ceremonies and dances, after which the newly captured heads were then prepared for various ceremonies. Often the hair would be cut off to decorate sword hilts and sheaths. The skulls were then smoked over a fire, and some tribes would carve decorative patterns into the skull's surface before the trophies were hung from the rafters of the longhouse.

FOOD PREP / EATING: Cooking fire + firewood; food storage in rafters above

TOILET: Enclosed toilet, located far from river to avoid contamination

WET AREA: Washing and bathing area; open to sky; rainwater collection area

ONE HOUSEHOLD

THE LONGHOUSE

POST & BEAM SYSTEM OF CONSTRUCTION:
The entire structure is built upon large ironwood piles (contains natural oils resistant to termite infestations), elevated above ground for added security, protection from floods and seismic activity, and to facilitate natural cooling. No nails are used throughout -- only traditional techniques of wood joinery and pegging.

FOUNDATIONS: In traditional longhouse construction, after the site is cleansed of any evil influences, various offerings are placed in the hole of the first post to be erected. These offerings would include the blood of a sacrificial cock, a riverstone to make the house "cool" (devoid of any intruding bad spirits), and the fluid in which the ritual leader's charms had been rinsed.

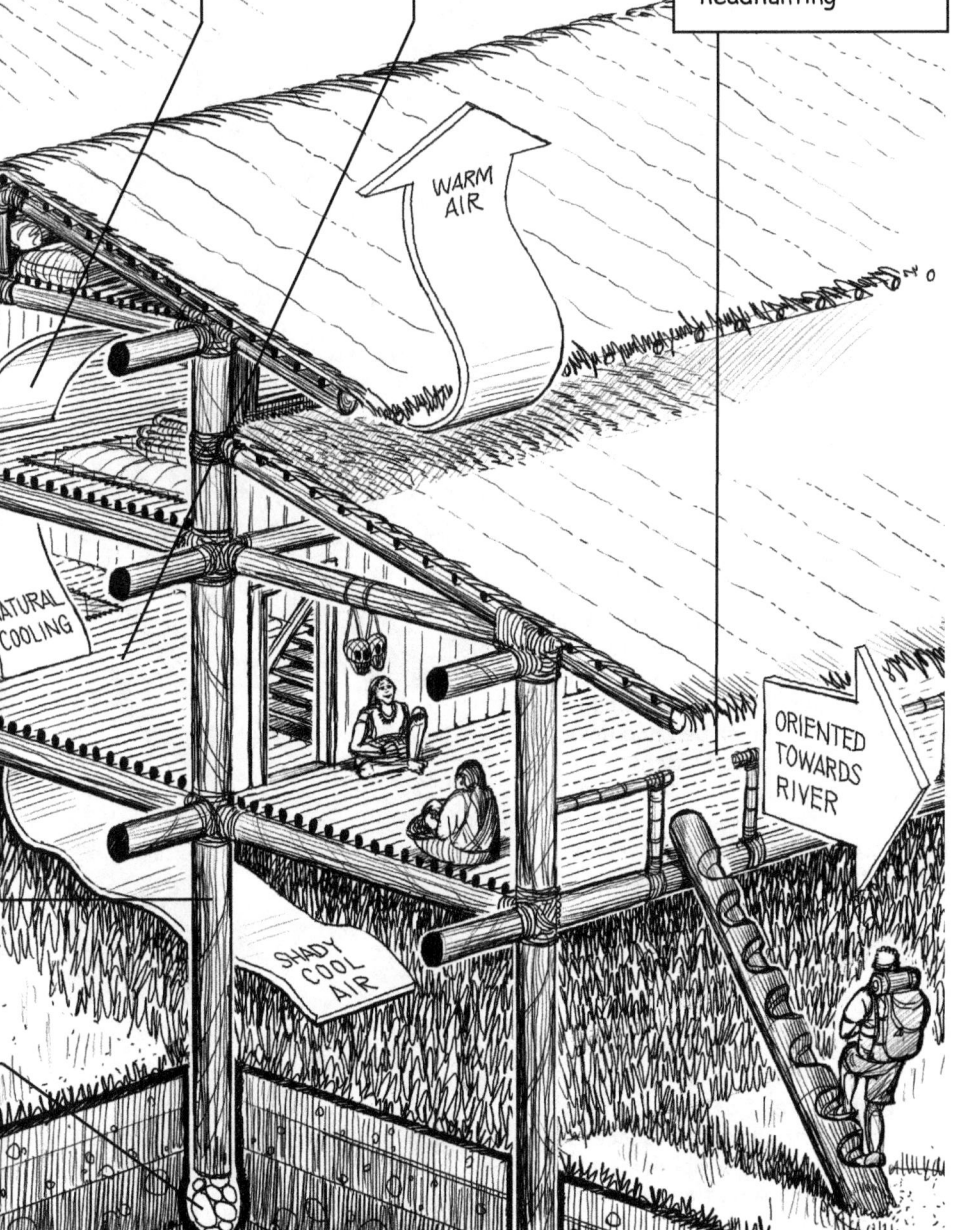

BORNEO TATTOOS

Tattooing ("tedek") in Borneo is often regarded as a spiritual art form that integrates living with spiritual beings. Renowned for their artistry, the Kayan were said to most heavily influence most tattoo designs found throughout Borneo.

The Kayan perfected the "woodblock stamp" technique, where men carved relief patterns into blocks of wood. These portable blocks were then smeared with black ink and transferred to the skin to provide a stencil for the tattoo. For the Kayan, the tattooist was typically a woman, possessing the skills and artistry passed down to her through heredity. Following the outline from the inked stencil, tattoos were hand-tapped using a hammer and bamboo splinters dipped in a dark pigment of soot, water, and sugar cane juice.

As it was widely thought that spirits embodied everything, many tattoos were patterned after plants or spirits with protective or curative powers. The resulting imagery included rosettes, dogs, frogs, scorpions, and shrimp. Some tribes had unique facial tattoos for easy identification in times of battle.

Kayan women were often adorned with tattoos from as early as eight years of age. In addition to serving as a mark of social standing and proof of their accomplishments in weaving, dancing, or singing; they also believed that the tattoos acted as "torches" to guide them through the darkness after death to the afterlife. For men, tattoos confirmed participation in successful headhunting raids, symbolized rites of passage, and sometimes served as proof of travel to distant lands.

DAY 10:

Our surreal adventure in this Kayan longhouse continued when my fellow travellers and I awoke to the sound of human howling and shrieking in the middle of the night.

After our brief introduction to headhunting the night before, we were all a bit on edge. I conferred with Ken and Jon early the next morning -- they had heard the screams as well. Our nervous host glanced around furtively and offered the explanation that the sounds were merely howling dogs.

We were offered a much-needed breakfast of fried rice to sooth our sour stomachs and pounding heads from a Borak drenched night of singing and dancing. We slowly packed our belongings and anxiously waited to see what was in store for us farther upriver. Ken and Jon had descended to the river for an early morning "mandi" (bath) while I began to reassemble the contents of my backpack.

Jim retreated to the upper level of the longhouse and soon returned with a small package wrapped in a leaf. He nervously gave this to me as a souvenir of our visit.

Unwrapping it, I found two small handcarvings. One item was a slender segment of bamboo that was intricately carved and decorated. The other item was a dark needle-like piece of wood. Jim explained that the tiny bamboo tube was a container in which Ibans would store important documents, and that the wood needle was an antique Kayan hairpin.

IBAN BAMBOO DOCUMENT HOLDER

- Carved by the Iban Dayak of Singgang, Sarawak (2nd div.) c. 1950

- Used for storing documents or other small tools

- Exterior of bamboo features red coloring referred to as "Dragon Blood" (red vegetable dye) obtained by grinding "mengkudu" (*movinda citrifolia*) root skin and mixing it with the inner bark of "djarabe" (*symplocos fanulata*). Alternatively, the red coloring can be obtained by using the red gummy sap of "angsana" (*pterocarpus indicus*)

KAYAN HAIR PIN

- Carved by the Kayan Dayak of Sarawak and used by women as a decorative hair pin

- Carved spirit on one end of the hair pin symbolizes protection

- Carved from a local hardwood known as "tampan" (an ironwood)

I thanked Jim profusely, but was embarrassed that I had nothing to give him in exchange. After emphasizing he expected nothing in return, came an explanation of the history of each artifact in detail, while I jotted down a few notes. He was strangely adamant that I keep these items secret from my fellow travellers, and urged me not to lose them. I cautiously accepted his gifts and wedged them into my backpack. Perhaps this was my "great reward."

Upon deciding to take a quick mandi in the river with the other longhouse residents, a completely nude Jon suddenly sprinted past me amidst choruses of laughter -- his sarong had been washed downstream while he was bathing!

After packing up, we were met with disappointment when Jim explained that he needed to continue his census recording work upstream alone, and that areas further upstream were not open to foreign visitors. It appeared that we were at the end of the line. He advised that we could either turn around and proceed back down the Rejang, or proceed overland to a town farther to the north via a series of uncharted logging roads. We put it to a vote and decided to explore the uncharted logging roads! We had gone this far; we decided to take another leap into the unknown.

Our trio soon found ourselves on the opposite bank of the river in the early morning light watching our mysterious host putter away upstream. We waved a groggy goodbye as we searched for a nearby logging road leading to a place called Tubau. Not having a plan, we had no idea where we were, nor did we have a map. What could be better?

08:37

Stranded on a dusty logging road, we wait for any type of vehicle to pass ...

08:46

... A passing land cruiser screeches to a halt, covering us in a blanket of dust. Joining three other locals, we hop in the back and fly down impossibly hilly roads at insane speeds ...

09:11

... Our ride drops us at a desolate timber collection area; we try to inquire about rides to Tubau while young macho loggers stare at us with an entrepreneurial gleam in their eyes. "No more transport today -- must charter our truck for many Ringgit ..."

We dash toward another passing logging truck and climb aboard for free -- we were on our way!

09:42

... Crunched in the tiny cab of a mammoth logging truck as an unblinking truck driver -- downshifting madly -- creeps up treacherously steep logging roads while hauling 34-tons of timber.

As we race downhill, he flips it into neutral, and we realize we are nothing more than a tiny metallic cart powered by a runaway 34-ton battering ram propelled from behind!

Death seemed imminent ...

11:55

... Our two-hour bumpy ride comes to an abrupt halt at a large logging camp. Our driver explains through a system of clever hand signals that we need to catch another truck heading to Tubau.

In less than one minute, we throw our packs onto the hitch of another truck, while climbing aboard to find a smiling dark-skinned driver ready to blast away to Tubau.

After several hours of roller coaster like dirt roads, we roll out of the steamy cab at the logging camp near Tubau, as the timber payload rolls off the truck with an earth-shattering crash ...

15:15

... We arrive at a riverside timber transfer station. We quickly discover the need to spend the night somewhere near Tubau as there are no more boats headed downstream to Bintulu for the day. We are quickly intercepted by a man beckoning us from a nearby riverboat. Sensing our predicament, he offers us a place to sleep for a few token Ringgit ...

15:31

... Exhausted, hungry, and extremely dusty, we accept the offer and tiptoe across a makeshift bridge of planks spanning an iridescent petrol-tainted river. After wolfing down noodles on a small supply boat, against our better judgment, we take a 10-second bath in the petrol tainted river to remove a day's layer of dust!

LOGGING IN SARAWAK:

Sarawak's rainforest is one of the oldest and biologically-rich ecosystems in the world, dating back 180 million years. As the world's largest exporter of tropical logs to the Japanese, Korean, and Taiwanese markets, many of Sarawak's key exports revolve around forest products.

Large scale logging in Sarawak began in the 1950s, and as early as 1985, almost half of the total forest area of Sarawak had reportedly been logged. Due to the unsustainable intensive logging practices of the past, there was now a strong emphasis on sustainable forest management. However, as is the case with many other rainforests around the world, problems with illegal logging operations still persist.

It was cited that in the past, for every tree that was cut down and sold, there was often an average of five corresponding trees that were damaged or left broken on the forest floor. This widespread loss of vegetation and serious soil erosion naturally resulted in increased silt loads and turbidity to streams in the affected areas during periods of rain, as well as the subsequent depletion of fish and wildlife depending upon those rivers for sustenance.

As a result, a rising tide of protests by indigenous forest-dwelling communities (most notably the nomadic hunter-gatherer tribe of the Penan) were identified by Malaysian and other international NGO's, as their reliance on forest-derived products sustaining their way of life (game, honey, rattan, fruit, medicines, building materials, etc.) became seriously jeopardized.

Despite the many opportunities for employment in the logging industry, this local resistance has resulted in timber blockades and clashes with logging companies as well as the government since the late 1980s. Many of the tribes have asserted that they have suffered a lack of consultation in logging activities, and have been barred access to their customary forest resources, which are rapidly disappearing. The once nomadic Penan and other indigenous peoples have been slowly pushed out of their ancestral forest homes, slowly losing the battle to big business.

DAY 11:

I emerged from a mosquito net covered with hundreds of varieties of insects. The supply shed where we had bedded down the previous night left much to be desired. We endured a hellish sleepless night trying to blot out a cacophony of screeching insects, a highly vocal family residing in a nearby hut, as well as a midnight chain saw competition somewhere upstream.

A misty morning revealed an express boat headed downstream. We made our way to the approaching boat across slippery rolling logs jammed against the riverbank.

Almost losing our feet between giant spinning logs, the three of us managed to throw ourselves upon the deck of the approaching boat.

By late morning, we had arrived in the coastal town of Bintulu. The three of us had collectively received recommendations from fellow travellers to visit the nearby Niah Caves.

A bumpy, dusty midday ride on a creaky school bus dropped us in Niah town. We were famished from the boat ride, and paused to devour a tasty serving of Mee Goreng and vegetables before catching a small boat up a ripple-free stagnant jungle river to the Niah Caves Park Hostel. Despite the communal sleeping room, the relaxed homey atmosphere of the hostel proved to be a sanctuary to recover from the past few days on the road. Our first task was to scrub the days of grime from our bodies and clothes.

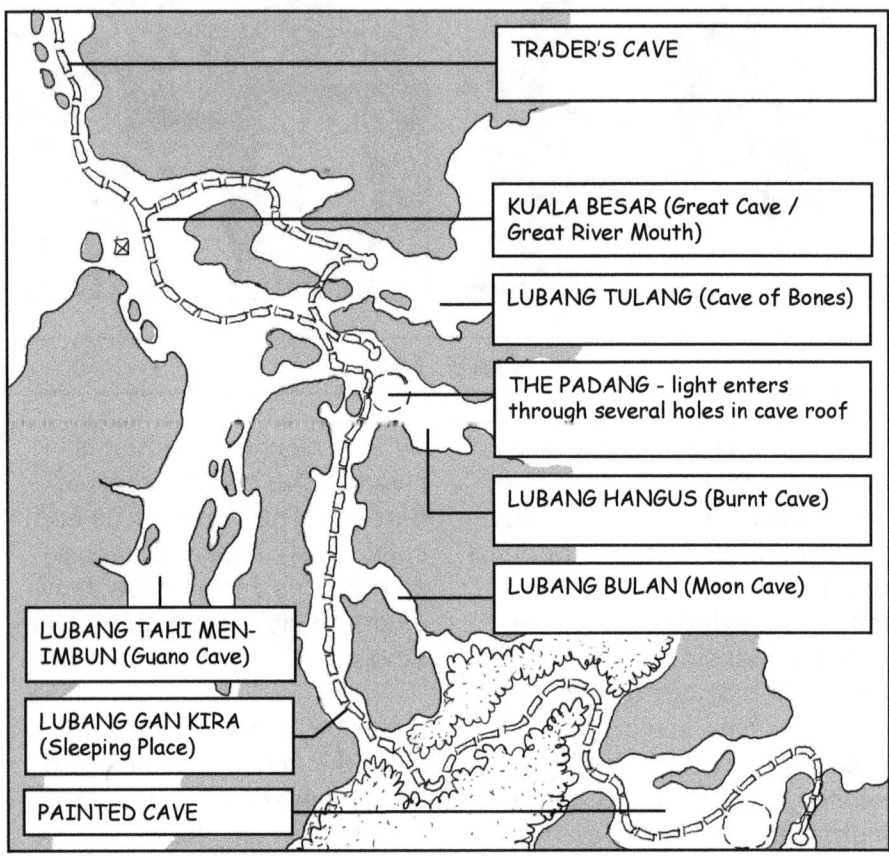

The complex of caves was supposedly within walking distance of the hostel, so in the last remaining hours of sunlight, we decided to explore.

Waving to a boatman across the river, an aggressive Ken negotiated a price and we soon found ourselves on a timber boardwalk on the opposite bank. We proceeded through dense jungle and around amazing rock formations covered with foliage. The face of the cliff soon opened as we proceeded through a large cavern open along one side -- the Trader's Cave -- featuring a massive opening framing views of the jungle beyond.

We paused here momentarily, and in the last minutes of remaining daylight, decided to forge ahead to the mouth of Kuala Besar -- the Great Cave.

A group of a dozen men ahead of us were busily constructing and erecting a tall pole secured by guy-wires. High in the upper reaches of this gargantuan cavern, a lone man teetered in total blackness atop a pieced-together bamboo pole, as he poked the roof of the cavern with another long piece of bamboo.

Like a circus act in the big top, this lone performer busily dislodged small birds' nests formed from the saliva of the hundreds of thousands of cave-dwelling swifts. The purveyors of this primary ingredient for the highly coveted "Bird's Nest Soup" found in fine Chinese restaurants everywhere, could reap a hefty profit.

It was rumored that the rampant extraction of nests had become so frequent, the swift populations had actually started to decline.

The bird nest collector's cohorts below surrounded him in a circle, knee deep in "guano" (bird and bat excrement); each concentrating the beams of their flashlights on the spectacle occurring 60 meters above. After a falling nest suddenly struck Ken's hat, one of the collectors cautiously approached us and explained that the Trader's Cave was where the birds' nest and guano traders conduct their business -- hence the name.

The sun had set. The noise level within the cavern gradually increased to a deafening pitch as two cohabitating species of winged creatures began their daily exchange.

The resident nocturnal bats soon began flocking out of dark corners of the cavern to begin their nocturnal hunt, as thousands of diurnal swifts returned to their nests for the night.

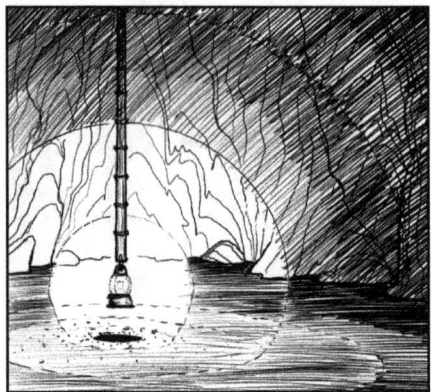 

Awestruck by this fantastic spectacle, we cautiously proceeded along a slippery guano encrusted boardwalk further into the bowels of the cavern.

Deeper inside, our world evolved into smaller glowing chambers containing suspended poles hanging vertically from the roof, each anchored with a small lantern to mark the site of these entrepreneurial nest collectors. We were told that this dangerous occupation was largely a family business that had been operating for generations.

Our presence was exposed by periodic blinding flashes of a collector's flashlight to illuminate and identify any interlopers.

We eventually walked full circle and returned to the mouth of the cave. Small blinking fireflies trailed past as we retraced our steps in the now black and chaotically alive jungle. My flashlight was transformed into a Jedi Knight's light saber as it cut through the evening mist.

A Canadian couple, whom we had briefly met inside the cave, called our attention to tiny phosphorescent mushrooms that glowed along the elevated boardwalk.

Strange trees appeared to move; visions of wild animals and perhaps still active headhunters arose from the medley of jungle sounds that surrounded us. Our imaginations ran wild as our eyes met with reflective night eyes staring up at us through the dense underbrush.

Even though it was evening, the humidity was close to 100%. We returned to the hostel and washed out our soaking clothes before collapsing into bed.

DAY 12:

The morning brought the disappointing news that the hostel was completely booked up for the evening. We packed our bags, leaving them at the ranger's office for the day, and planned to spend the afternoon exploring the wondrous Niah Caves further.

As we returned to the Great Cave from the night before, the daylight now illuminated vibrant shades of green covering the rock formations near the entrance of this vast cavern complex.

We had learned from the helpful hostel staff that the Niah Caves' primary claim to fame is that of being one of the earliest examples of civilization in the region. The oldest modern human remains discovered in Southeast Asia were found at Niah, making the park one of the most important archaeological sites in the world. It was said that in 1958, a skull was unearthed which was estimated to be 40,000 years old!

Jon, Ken, and I proceeded down a boardwalk past a modern timber structure, completely dwarfed by the towering cavern walls. We continued over a traversing set of timber stairs to another chamber: The Padang.

This chamber was illuminated by a brilliant shaft of sunlight beaming down from an aperture high above. We continued on into a smaller, darker, tubular cave containing huge colorless crickets and tiny scorpions that scuttled between the slats of the boardwalk. Jon began sneezing uncontrollably.

 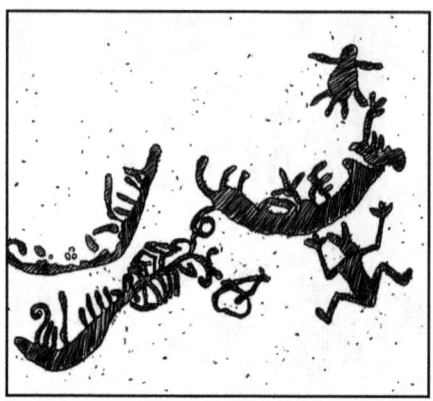

I hurriedly tiptoed through the menacing scorpions below, and switched off my flashlight, as I shot a glance back at the groups of nest collectors from the night before. They were now huddled in small circles in various dark corners of this bizarre nocturnal world, as we entered the land of sunshine once again.

A ten-minute stroll through lowland forest teeming with birds and butterflies brought us to the entrance of yet another cave. The Painted Cave was said to be embellished with prehistoric cave paintings dating back to the first century A.D.

A visit here was supposedly only permissible with a permit. We didn't have one. There was not a soul around, so we reluctantly entered this expanse of darkness and stumbled ahead.

After our eyes adjusted to the darkness, we had split up to search for the prehistoric dark red paintings.

Jon yelped "I found them!" as we rushed to his side. Rendered in red hematite, the prehistoric images depicted boats, scorpion-like creatures, and dancing figures. It was said that some of these images represented warriors and hunters that were buried here, as evidenced by the various "death ships" that had been discovered on the cave floor some years before.

These boat-shaped coffins, dating back to AD 780, had apparently contained the remains of the deceased and a variety of items considered useful in the afterlife, such as ceramics, ornaments and glass beads. I had recalled seeing the contents of some of these death ships back at the Sarawak Museum in Kuching.

I was in awe as I studied these 2,000-year old paintings. The span of my own life seemed so insignificant at that moment in time.

As we began to retrace our steps, Ken spotted a narrow crevice that descended quite steeply. Ken, who spent most of his waking hours in claustrophobic mines, beckoned us to follow him as he gripped a nearby ledge and swung down into the chasm.

The three of us carefully descended this narrow precipice with Jon bringing up the rear; the air became more foul and dank with each step into the unknown.

Ken, who had sped ahead with excitement, had reached a small underground river. After regrouping, we scanned the surface above us. We found a black furry cavern ceiling covered with sleeping inverted winged beasts. It was one of those moments where I didn't know whether to freeze or flee. Our glaring flashlights soon sent a wave of bats vibrating and blinking as the cavern filled with ultrasonic screeches.

"Let's get the hell out of here!" someone screamed. Falling over one another, we leapt out of the precipice, fell into a foul-smelling pile of guano, and sprinted out into the jungle as the screeching subsided. The sun had set, we were covered in bat crap, and we had nowhere to sleep.

We returned to the hostel, and owing to a few cancellations -- we now had a place to spend the night! Our elation subsided when we were quickly escorted to the showers before being admitted back into the dormitory. Ken cursed as he was asked to burn some of his foul-smelling clothes.

Our peaceful vegetative state on the verandah of the Niah Park Hostel that evening was suddenly disrupted ...

Two of five Canadian women that were staying at the hostel came running up -- drenched with sweat -- from a sunset stroll in the jungle.

They explained that three members of their group had wandered off the trail and had not yet returned before sundown. The two survivors were absolutely panic-stricken as they raced around and assembled a nonsensical seven-day supply of chocolate bars, and 20-30 spare flashlight batteries for an all-night search party.

An elderly hostel guest of Indian descent waved a finger and warned, "It's not the animals I'm worried about ... it's the men!" This remark sent the two breathless surviving women into a tailspin as they pleaded for us to join them in their search and rescue operation.

We sprung to our feet, hurriedly packed some food and water, and smeared on a lethal dose of DEET mosquito repellent. We split up into two search parties, and the Park Ranger had assembled a fleet of canoes to search downriver.

Then, at the last minute, three puzzled women emerged from the jungle. Sensing a crisis, they quickly volunteered to join the search party -- not knowing that it was organized to find them!

DAY 13:

The "lost" Canadians from the previous night had persuaded us to visit Gunung Mulu National Park while we were in Sarawak. We each only had 30-day visas, but we collectively decided it was best to see as much as we could, and as cheaply as possible, within our allotted time. Perhaps Gunung Mulu was the location of my "great reward."

Jon concluded, "I'm so tired of fried noodles," as we waited in a Niah Town cafe for the bus to Miri -- our first stepping-stone in the journey to Gunung Mulu.

The bus finally rolled up an hour late. A crowd of people, who had been previously striking nonchalant poses in various stores and cafes surrounding the town square, madly raced toward the bus, clambered aboard, and elbowed us out of the way. We stood in a steamy packed bus for 20 minutes before any motion ensued. Small children were packed in like sardines, chickens clucked from within flimsy cardboard boxes, and anyone left standing tried to grasp anything stationary as the bus heaved back and forth, rolling to life.

A pothole-filled dusty road finally gave way to a paved road, and two hours later we had reached the town of Miri. Dazed and confused after a jolting journey, we lumbered through town in search of a bed for the night. We meandered from one cheap hotel to another, while Ken griped, "Geez, these guidebook maps are really out of date." Jon countered, "Do you always complain so much?"

We all were tired and desperate for a clean room and a hot shower. The first few hotels we had come across looked like they had not been cleaned in ten years. We surmised the cockroaches far outnumbered the guests at some of these inns.

Moving from one roach motel to another, we finally came across a shockingly clean hotel lobby -- almost to the point of being sterilized. We ascended the stairway of this seemingly promising hotel, following the elderly proprietor, to inspect the rooms on offer.

The strong stench of cheap perfume filled the hotel, as we passed several rooms with scantily dressed women poised in various doorways. Ken's eyes lit up, as Jon and I exchanged uncertain glances. The proprietor reassured us, "No problem, this floor not hotel -- hotel upstairs!"

We ascended one more flight of stairs to the "hotel floor" as the winking girls made beckoning motions. Despite our better judgment, the very economical rooms, available by the hour, appeared absolutely spotless and they had hot water! We accepted.

We had each retired to our respective rooms for a hot shower, which is one of those unappreciated luxuries until you go without. Looking forward to a very restful night sleep, I did a quick batch of hand washed laundry and draped clothing over various furnishings to dry overnight.

As I sat on the bed, I was greeted by a peculiar crackling sound. Upon pulling back the bed sheets covering a stained mattress, to my horror there were dozens of cockroaches and smaller insects scurrying across the bedding!

I cursed loud enough to attract Jon's attention through the paper thin walls, who tapped on my door just seconds later. I quickly pointed out my discovery and postulated that his bed might also be already occupied by another non-paying guest.

We instantly agreed the quest for suitable accommodation must continue. Finding Ken, we quickly regrouped, packed up, and quickly dashed down to the hotel lobby. The proprietor was kind enough to refund our deposit, despite having showered.

Continuing our search for accommodation, we tried someplace completely different: The Miri Red Crescent Society. A few Ringgit could buy one night on a mattress on the floor of a stifling upstairs room occupied by a Punan family and a friendly group of Muslim school teachers.

After each claiming an available mattress, we were soon accosted by one of the teachers sporting a tightly-wrapped black turban; he displayed an amazing propensity for talking. We chatted briefly as they brought us up on the local news. In Kuching, one of Sarawak Museum's prized exhibits on loan had suddenly been withdrawn by its owner. In fact, it was the same curious Easter Island artifact I had noted during my visit. That was a coincidence, or was it?

Our conversation led to an invitation to a communal meal with seven turbaned friends at an excellent Islamic restaurant. We feasted on a variety of fabulous dishes, a welcome departure from our staple of Mee Goreng. The teachers explained that our Halal meal consisted of permissible dishes under Islamic law.

During a pleasant stroll around town after our meal, our group of three Westerners decided a beer or two would be in order after the day's events.

Our Muslim friends respectfully declined the offer for a beer. As they continued back to the Red Crescent Society for the night, we found ourselves at the top of a rickety outdoor staircase hidden in a nondescript side street.

The door swung open revealing a darkened smoke-filled lounge. A live band from the Philippines gyrated beneath an eerie orange light on a small stage in the corner of the club.

This color coordinated group of seven performers smiled and swayed, as they sang sentimental love songs. The lead singer was a vision of beauty and kept shooting flirtatious glances our way.

During the band's break, a video Karaoke system was activated. The attractive lead singer joined our table along with some of her band mates. She unravelled tales of the hardship that many Filipino bands need to endure working overseas for scant amounts of money and often abusive conditions. As Ken snuggled up to this "damsel in distress," we were compelled to buy the band a round of beers.

During the band's next break, they urged us to sing Karaoke songs. I scrawled out the name of a timeless Beatles tune on a scrap of paper, and in no time, our group of scruffy travellers were churning out embarrassing renditions of classic songs. The club obviously did not receive many foreign visitors; the crowd applauded enthusiastically despite our dismal attempts at singing. A much needed night of fun!

DAY 14:

My sheets were drenched with sweat as I rolled sideways to life that morning. I had groggy memories of Ken staying behind at the bar the night before. The stifling room at the Miri Red Crescent Society prompted Jon and me to indulge in a refreshingly cool shower -- but Ken was nowhere to be found.

After dressing, our Aussie cohort abruptly walked through the door and announced, "G'day! Let's get some brekkie, mates." While we devoured several tasty roti canai at a noisy cafe, Jon and I quizzed Ken about his absence throughout the night. A smiling Ken gloated, "Sorry mates, I don't kiss and tell."

We decided that nearby Lambir National Park sounded like it could be an interesting day trip. An economical bus ride brought us to a boardwalk leading to a favored picnic spot. Relaxing and watching dozens of squealing children splashing beneath a gentle waterfall, we later climbed the "Panau Tree Tower." This 40-meter high timber staircase was constructed around a solitary tree which afforded visitors with a prime bird-watching treetop vantage point. After strolling through other sections of the park, we thought it best to return to town before sundown. We soon found ourselves beneath a blazing afternoon sun with no way of returning to Miri.

Impatient, and in an effort to beat the heat, we decided to try hitchhiking. After only three passing cars, a 4-wheel drive vehicle swerved over to our rescue.

The driver who had picked us up was an expat of indeterminate origin who worked in neighboring Brunei on an offshore oil rig. He drove furiously while guzzling a can of beer, and complained incessantly about the lack of his favorite alcoholic beverage in a tiny country he described as claustrophobic. He had been transferred to Brunei through his company, but escaped across the border to a more free-wheeling Miri whenever given the chance.

After his tirade, we thanked him for the lift, as he dropped us back in Miri. We embarked on a leisurely stroll through the late afternoon heat, but were soon caught up in a bustling Chinese funeral procession. After being jostled around and ensconced in clouds of incense, we escaped the noisy crowds into the shade of a nearby building arcade.

Within the busy arcade, crouched on a rattan mat, a man waved us over to inspect his wares. He handed Ken a small photo album containing images of a dead crocodile and the bloody remnants of a small boy that the beast had tried to devour. He then proudly produced a dried, shrivelled, root-like object that he professed to be the crocodile's penis!

He then pointed out a collection of small glass vials of yellow oil containing tiny shreds of the crocodile penis that could be made available for a "special price." He asserted that this wonder oil could be applied externally for mosquito bites and deep muscle pain, or taken internally to increase libido. He quickly produced a doctor-endorsed certificate of authenticity from a briefcase as Ken rubbed his chin and nodded. Ken bought two vials out of curiosity.

DAY 15:

The morning was spent running around town and collecting permits for travel to Gunung Mulu National Park: a typical procedure of racing between several government offices on a scavenger hunt collecting scraps of illegible forms and stamps from unbelievably apathetic clerks. We completed this process in the hour before we caught a bus to Kuala Baram on the Baram River.

Once again avoiding the irritating Kung-Fu videos within an icy air-conditioned boat interior, we perched ourselves atop the luggage rack of an express boat travelling upriver to Marudi. I baked in the sun and cast a lazy stare at men reclined in hammocks on a weathered craft chugging the opposite direction downriver, as they towed a forest or two of felled trees behind them. With visions of superhuman virility, Ken cracked open one of the crocodile penis oil vials, threw its contents down his throat, and beamed with pride.

We soon arrived in Marudi. Situated on the banks of the Baram River, this riverside town was home to Fort Hose, an outpost from the Brooke era. Our initial foray into Marudi was marked by sitting in the first restaurant we came across to satisfy our hunger, followed by collectively figuring out our next steps. While discussing our options, Ken suddenly grimaced, leapt up, and frantically tried to find a toilet. But it was too late. A dark brown frothy liquid ran down his legs -- the crocodile penis oil had taken it's revenge!

"Allo!" came a voice from behind. We were approached by a colorfully dressed German backpacker named Franz whom we had seen from afar in Miri. As one does travelling independently, he joined our table, and we were soon a group of four in search of a place to spend the night. I stayed behind and watched the packs, while Jon and Franz made the rounds through the center of town. Ken was moaning in the toilet.

After settling on a small shared room above a Chinese dry goods store, we retreated to a neighboring restaurant for a meal of curried meats and vegetables, while Ken convalesced for the evening in the foul-smelling toilet. At the restaurant, we discovered Franz had a penchant for cooking, as he invited himself into the kitchen to see what kind of spices and curry powders were on hand.

Franz reminded me of a character out of a film. He was on a culinary odyssey as he rattled off the destinations he had visited before our chance encounter. He began pulling tightly-wrapped packets of herbs and spices from his pack that he had collected from his travels.

"Und zis," he continued, "Is verboten in Germany," as he erupted in hysterical laughter. Revisiting the kitchen, he shortly returned to our table with yet more samples of local spices to add to his collection.

After dinner, Franz suggested we have a "nightcap." We found ourselves in yet another Karaoke bar, located in a dimly lit second-story lounge. Retiring early to rest for our final stretch to Gunung Mulu, we drifted off to sleep enjoying some soft jazz which Franz played through a pair of portable speakers.

DAY 16:

We arose to loud shouts in a Chinese dialect emanating from the dry goods store below our room. After realizing the bellowing was normal conversation and not a warning of impending doom, we quickly packed and descended to the store below and purchased provisions for the next few days.

At the last minute, running to the jetty toting bags stuffed with canned foods and water, we leapt onto the only boat departing upstream that day. This crowded craft also shuttled two effeminate Dutch men clad in matching brand-name outfits. They gloated for hours about the "luxuriousness" of their well organized package tour and looked at us with pure disdain. Smiling fiendishly, Ken offered them a vial of "croc oil."

We were soon transferred to a smaller longboat farther upriver containing locals, as the Dutch Duo, with their matching eye wear, sped by in their modern speedboat smirking and winking. Ken returned a sarcastic smile as Jon nudged me and whispered, "maybe this is your great reward," and chuckled.

Jon's comment was a haunting reminder of my cryptic note. I had started to give up hope of receiving a "reward."

After a marathon eight-hour journey of pushing our tiny boat through waist-deep rapids, the empathetic boat owner, Paul, offered us a place to stay at his small canteen located near the fully-booked Mulu Park Headquarters. As usual, we had no reservations anywhere.

Upon arriving at Paul's stilted riverside canteen, we were famished. We had paid Paul a token amount for a few makeshift beds on the floor. At least it was a roof over our heads.

Our stomachs growling, we each withdrew our trusty Swiss Army knives. Ken, Jon, and I furiously sliced and diced a variety of vegetables we had bought in Marudi. Franz orchestrated the concoction of a bubbling, seasoned, mystery stew as he pranced around adding various amounts of spices that he had accumulated during the last couple of years of travelling the world.

The resulting stew was surprisingly good, as we each sipped warm Anker Beers. After Ken confessed that he had chopped off a chunk of his fingernail in the preparation of this homemade meal, we discussed the next steps of our journey with Paul the boat owner.

Franz had specifically come to Gunung Mulu to climb the famous limestone "pinnacles," which he kept mispronouncing. He explained that the pinnacles were a series of 45-meter high, razor-sharp limestone spikes that towered above the surrounding vegetation, along the slopes of Gunung Api. A steep hike not for the faint-hearted.

He estimated that the limestone karst formations were the only remnants of a previously continuous limestone bed, which had become eroded by the forces of nature over thousands of years. Franz rubbed his hands together as he howled, "Pineapples, here we come!" A nearby electric generator produced a soothing, hypnotic purr that swept us away for the night.

DAY 17:
Gunung Mulu National Park

We kicked off the morning with a pleasantly smooth boat ride in a tiny longboat up the river to the Park Headquarters. We had discovered that the ascent up the limestone pinnacles was going to be more costly than anticipated. Alternatively, an ascent up the summit of Gunung Mulu (no boats involved) would be cheaper -- we were faced with a decision.

Arriving at the Park Headquarters, we opted to explore two caves within walking distance. Paying the compulsory guide fee, we crept along a 3 km. boardwalk that snaked its way through the rainforest, while soaking up the sights and sounds of this fantastic ecosystem -- amazing plant life, insects that resembled tree branches, and eerie ultrasonic chirps from unseen creatures!

We waited for what could have been two hours at the entrance of the Deer Cave until a guide showed up. This immensely huge cave (and yet one of the smaller caves in the park) contained an astonishing variety of muted colors deep within its interior. It was said to be home to over 13 million bats consisting of three different species. Our guide spotted a disabled bat (a wingspan of perhaps 20 cm) and stretched the wings of the black writhing cave-dweller beneath our flashlights. The blinding flash of a passing French tourist's camera sent the creature spinning before it sank its needle like teeth into our guide's finger!

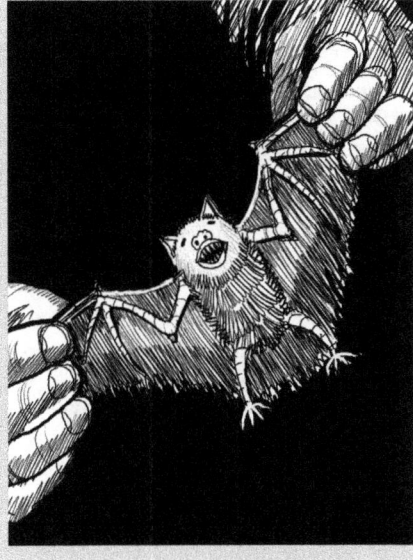

GUNUNG MULU NATIONAL PARK

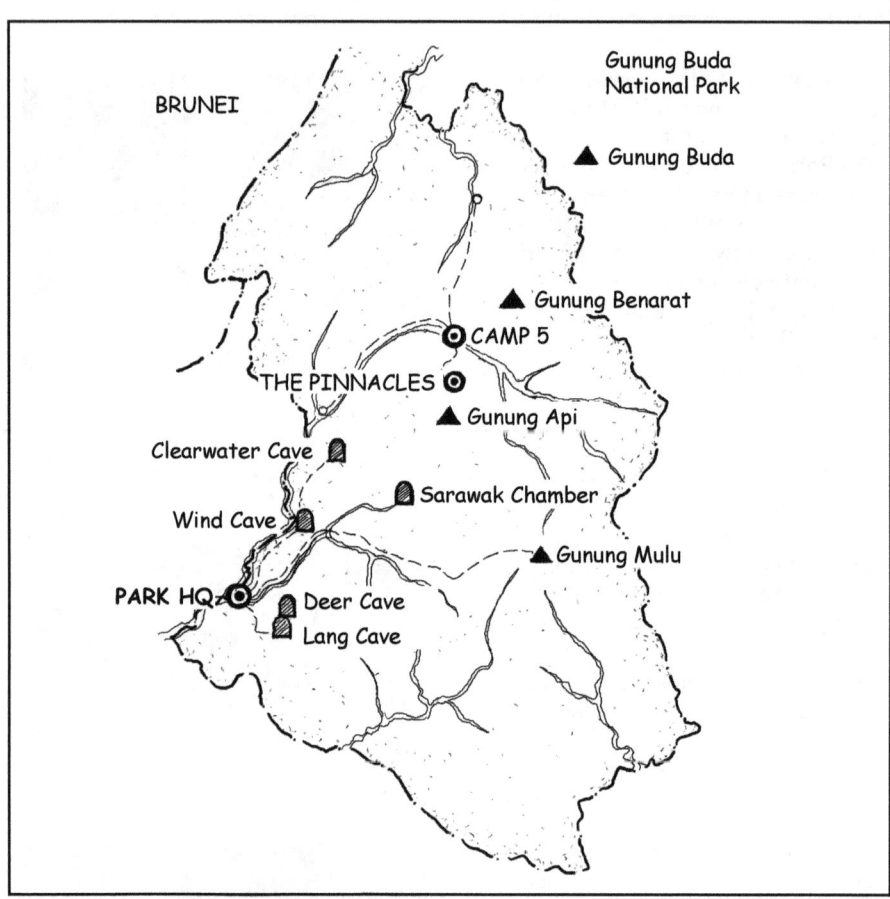

Designated a World Heritage Site in 2000, **Gunung Mulu National Park** occupies an area of almost 544 sq. km. -- almost the size of Singapore. The Park is dominated by the 2,377 m. high Gunung Mulu (Mt. Mulu), the second highest mountain in Sarawak.

Geologically, the mountains are composed of various slates and hard sandstones ranging from 40 - 60 million years old. To the west of Gunung Mulu lies the lower peaks of Gunung Api and Gunung Benarat, which comprise the Melinau Limestone Formation. Within these water soluble and porous limestone mountains, an extensive cave system was formed over two million years that consists of hundreds of caves, only 70 of which (totalling 300 km) have been surveyed by various caving expeditions. Only a handful of caves are open to the general public. Situated almost 1 km. above the base of Gunung Api and Benarat are the famous "pinnacles" -- pointed sharp-edged limestone daggers that rise above the surrounding treetops to a height of 45 m. The adjacent 62 sq. km. **Gunung Buda National Park** was founded in 1996 to extend the park system further northward.

GUNUNG MULU NATIONAL PARK

FLORA & FAUNA:

Gunung Mulu National Park is home to equatorial rainforest that feature an amazing biological diversity. In addition to all the major inland vegetation types of Borneo, Mulu features a wide variety of forests ranging from peat swamps to upper montane vegetation at the mountain's summit.

To date, Gunung Mulu is known to contain thousands of types of fungi and plant species, in addition to hundreds of species of mammals, frogs, and fish.

A staggering 170 species of wild orchids as well as insect-eating "pitcher plants" can be found here. The insects are especially diverse and abundant, and include almost 300 species of butterflies and almost 500 species of ants. Every day at dusk, some of the caves are the site of an incredible simultaneous migration of millions of nocturnal bats streaming out of the cave, while the diurnal cave-dwelling swallows and swifts return into the cave for the night -- at exactly the same time!

SELECT "SHOW" CAVES:

Clearwater Cave:
With over 150 km. of discovered passages, the Clearwater Cave is the longest cave system in Southeast Asia. Its primary attraction is its cool clear underground stream, rated as one of the finest underground rivers of the world.

Wind Cave:
The Wind Cave is noted for its unusual calcite formations and its cool drafts of air -- hence the name. Within one of its chambers, known as the "King's Room," the speleothems (see below) are said to resemble chandeliers and candlesticks.

Deer Cave:
The Deer Cave is a through passage, featuring two huge entrances. One of the openings, at 100 m wide and 120 m high, once had the distinction of being the largest cave passage known to mankind. The Deer Cave is also the home of the world's largest bat colony.

Lang Cave:
The Lang Cave is one of the smaller caves open to the public and contains some of the most intricate textures of any of the Mulu caves within its interior.

Sarawak Chamber:
Discovered only in 1980, the majestic Sarawak Chamber is one of the world's largest chambers, measuring an estimated 600 m long, 400 m wide, and 100 m high. This cave contains the world's largest natural underground chamber, and is frequently partially filled with water.

Stalactites & Stalagmites:
Formed over tens of thousands of years, "speleothem" are accumulations of various calcium-based precipitates. Resembling melted candle wax, speleothem include "stalactites" (pointed pendants hanging from the cave ceiling), "stalagmites" (bluntly pointed mounds on the cave floor, often beneath stalactites), and "columns" (when stalactites and stalagmites meet).

On our way out of the Deer Cave, we encountered a large group of Chinese chattering away, shovelling rice out of a portable rice cooker. They invited us to join their spontaneous cave-side picnic and sample some of their rice before proceeding to the Lang Cave. The Chinese gentleman was adamant that the Chinese are habitually worried they will run out of food, so they carry their own food with them at all times.

We thanked the Chinese family for the pleasant snack and proceeded to the adjacent Lang Cave. This damp, intimate cavern featured unbelievable drippy stalagmite and stalactite formations that had gradually formed over millions of years.

At sunset, we retreated to the Bat Observatory building to witness the daily exodus of bats from the mouth of the Deer Cave. A few random swarms of black specks shot forth from the depths of the cave, later combining to produce an otherworldly swirling corkscrew-like stream miles long that slowly dissipated as it reached the depths of the surrounding jungle.

I was convinced that my dreams would be tainted with imagery from a well-known Alfred Hitchcock film that night. We returned to the Park Headquarters where we had reserved beds in a shared room, later spending the evening at the Mulu Pub, a covered verandah next to the Mulu Canteen. After securing a boat for tomorrow's journey, we chatted with some attractive local park guides until 2 am ... Ken stayed much longer.

DAY 18:
Gunung Mulu National Park

A late night at the Mulu Pub left the four of us yearning for an extra few hours of sleep. We hurriedly packed our daypacks in order to catch our boat up to the trail leading to the spiky Pinnacles. Stuffing a minimal assortment of personal effects into daypacks, we left the bulk of our things in our larger backpacks at the Park Headquarters. The boat pulled up, and like a scene out of a movie, the moment we started down the gangplank leading to the boat, buckets of rain began to fall!

Hoping this was just a brief downpour, we continued upriver with ten other tourists. We were reunited with the Dutch Duo, who clad in their sparkling white T-shirts, greatly contrasted with my muddy-river-water-stained shirt that was becoming more wet from the jungle precipitation. They were no longer smiling; perhaps they too had sampled Ken's oil!

After waiting in the pouring rain, we soon discovered that there were no more Pinnacle guides who could be hired that day -- but we had already paid Paul the boatman for the boat ride up and back! So there we were: no money, the boat had left upriver with the other tourists, we were soaked from the torrential rain, we had no Pinnacle guide, and finally someone had confiscated our permits at the Park Headquarters, vanishing shortly thereafter.

What would we do now?

After venting our collective frustrations, we decided to make the best of the situation. We decided to revisit the Deer and Lang Caves in more detail. As we were already soaked, we trudged without ponchos through a misty jungle in the rain. A rather apathetic guide delivered us to the Bat Observation building that was brimming with package tour members.

We were pleasantly surprised when we were befriended by an older bearded tourist from Sri Lanka. He must have taken pity on our disheveled appearance as he offered us his lunch of fried rice and noodles that was included in his tour; for some reason, it was not particularly to his liking.

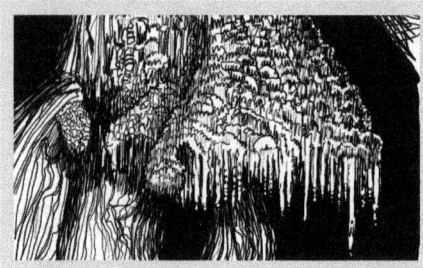

After thanking our culinary benefactor, we continued on for a second visit to the Lang Cave. This time, additional strategically-located spotlights were activated, revealing fantastic calcium encrusted formations. After gazing at this natural masterpiece, we proceeded back to the Deer Cave.

We had persuaded our guide to lead us across slippery guano covered boulders into the "Garden of Eden" portion of the cavern. Traversing across huge mountains of foul-smelling bat excrement created by the squeaky inhabitants above, we circled around "Adam's Shower" -- a curious shower head shaped stalactite from which water cascaded down around its perimeter -- hence the name. After a day of cave exploration, we checked into the nearby Melinau Canteen for the night.

DAY 19:
Gunung Mulu National Park

After a wonderful night's sleep at the Melinau Canteen, we arose to find Paul, the boatman whom we had previously paid for the Pinnacle trip, waiting to bring us upriver. Stocking up on a supply of food, we puttered up to the Park Headquarters and were issued our compulsory native guide, Andrew, as well as a silent muscle bound Italian travelling magician who called himself "Stefano the Great."

We were slightly disappointed to find that Andrew ("Oh yes, all of our guides speak fluent English") communicated almost solely in Malay. Our first stop upriver was the Clearwater Cave, which boasted a "spectacular boat ride through one of the longest cave systems in Southeast Asia." Andrew's response was: "No today, water too low."

As we headed upriver, our quota of exercise was filled by jumping out of the boat every five minutes and pushing it up the rapids in a river that was already abnormally low. Did we really need a boat?

Just before the 27th exodus from the boat to help push, I stepped out over the edge into the cool mountain water up to my knee, up to my waist, up to my neck ... I watched the boat and its laughing occupants fade away as I was mercilessly swept downstream. Managing to swim ashore, I hiked along the riverbank and rejoined the boatload of giggling travellers.

I was now completely soaked. This was soon of little consequence when the sky turned to liquid. A short rain shower was enough to drench the rest of us thoroughly. After three hours of pushing the boat upriver, we had arrived at the trail leading to Camp 5, the first step in ascending the Pinnacles.

As the sun would soon be setting, we quickly wrung the water out of our clothes and laced up our hiking boots. We rambled through dense jungle along a barely discernible path. We were warned to pull up our socks for protection from blood-sucking leeches.

Already tired and hiking in damp clothes, we were soon besieged by a horrendous downpour. My waterproof rain poncho was totally inaccessible, as it was buried at the bottom of my daypack. Not good planning. Stefano ripped off his wet shirt, and sped ahead.

LEECH ALERT! After the rain, some of us had discovered small writhing blood-suckers affixed to our legs that had inescapably brushed by wet plants along the path. These slimy slinky creatures implanted themselves firmly upon our legs and could not be pulled off! But they could be sizzled off with a disposable lighter!

After a thorough leech check, we continued along the path which had now transformed into a muddy torrent. After much slipping and sliding, we eventually came upon a clearing containing several deserted rudimentary structures. We had arrived: Camp 5.

One small covered timber structure was raised from the ground and had a cooking area; slightly better than I had envisioned. My waterproof trekking boots were squishing with water when I had arrived, but at least I was free of leeches. Jon wasn't so lucky; he had a gaping wound on his inner thigh that would not stop bleeding.

My only set of clothes was totally soaked, the sun had set, and we were all famished. We cooked up a large batch of Nasi Goreng that Paul our boatman had thoughtfully wrapped in a banana leaf. Even in the face of adversity, Franz the gourmet had somehow managed to bring a stash of secret spices to perk up our meal.

I hung my clothes to dry from a clothesline strung from the cobweb covered rafters of our hut and borrowed Ken's dry sarong in which to sleep. Ironically, the only dry item in my pack was my plastic rain poncho, which I employed as a sheet that night. As the fire died down, we tried to communicate with our guide, Andrew. His English was not sufficient to hold a conversation, and our Bahasa was even worse. It was then "Stefano the Great" disappeared into the jungle, never to be seen again.

Guessing this was all part of his disappearing act, I retired for the night and dreamt of leeches as I shivered wrapped in my rain poncho. This was a good lesson in being prepared. What happened to my Boy Scout training as a youngster? Would I even make it to the top of the Pinnacles at this rate? Was this my great reward?

THE PINNACLES
Gunung Mulu National Park

DAY 20:
Gunung Mulu National Park

A sleepless night finally ended when our guide rousted my frozen body out of bed. My clothes were still very damp, and now very cold. We threw our damp clothes near the morning fire. Devouring a breakfast of instant noodles, Jon raced to the fire too late to find a deformed, melted hiking boot.

We had a cloudless morning as I slid on my still damp clothes. Pulling up my socks from leech paranoia, our guide assured us that the higher limestone forest we were about to enter would be devoid of such lowland nightmares.

We began to ascend a steep slope of jagged rocks. As the slope increased, I sweated profusely while my heart began to race. Our guide effortlessly sped ahead. Following trees marked with red paint dots, the terrain soon turned into limestone cliffs only navigable by using fixed ropes and ladders between certain precipices.

After three hours, Jon, with his disabled boot, was the last to reach the summit of a massive rock outcropping that overlooked a valley of amazing needle-like limestone pinnacles jutting up from the lush green rainforest below. The views were exhilarating. Drying our clothes on sunny rocks, we paused for a few group photos to mark our successful ascent up the razor sharp Pinnacles. Suddenly, Stefano appeared from behind a rock, took a bow, and vanished.

We reluctantly began our journey back down, which proved more treacherous and strenuous than the ascent. My legs quickly turned to rubber as I flailed down the mountainside, swinging on vines, and tripping on tree roots.

Upon our return to Camp 5, I collapsed from exhaustion and nibbled on a chocolate bar to revive myself. I peeled off my sweat-drenched clothing and wandered down to the nearby cool river -- a small slice of heaven!

After gazing up at the Pinnacles we had just ascended and hanging my damp clothing to dry in the last few hours of sunlight, I rejoined the group at the communal Camp 5 picnic table. We chatted with a recently arrived group of travellers, including a chatty Australian couple, a couple from France that refused to converse, and a giggling group of Malaysians.

As the sun disappeared, the light from the cooking fire illuminated our table while we prepared yet another batch of Nasi Goreng in the crusty Camp 5 wok. We stuffed our faces with a curried concoction of fried rice, onions, ginger, corn, and beans.

Stefano inexplicably reappeared from the jungle, as one Chinese gentleman from the group of Malaysians retired for the evening. An irregular melody of snores and grunts made a rapid descent into dreamland difficult, but my sheer exhaustion drew my eyes closed for another night on a bamboo mat covering an uneven wood floor.

DAY 21:
Gunung Mulu National Park

My bladder was ready to burst upon waking in the early morning. I followed the familiar path leading to the Camp 5 outhouse -- a treacherous smelling structure with a square hole in the floor. I later returned to a smoky fire and cooked up our last packets of instant noodles.

That morning the silent "Stefano the Great" went missing once again; the guide simply shrugged his shoulders. Packing up our rubbish, we began retracing our steps through the leech-infested jungle. My vision soon became transfixed on the obstacle course that passed beneath my feet.

After 90 minutes of trudging through damp jungle and intensely scanning trail side vegetation to evade swaying leeches, we reached our longboat. After a thorough leech check, we scrambled onto the longboat and cast off downstream. Stefano had disappeared.

My legs were still sore from the Pinnacle hike the day before; luckily the trip downstream involved less pushing -- but we all became soaked nonetheless. Franz grinned as he repeatedly chanted, "Yah, I have conquered zee Pineapples!" We were enthralled by the sheer variety of life and range of sounds around us as we floated downriver through lush rainforest, and over intermittent rapids. We made a few unplanned stops due to Ken's distressed digestive system.

As we neared the Gunung Mulu Park Headquarters, we had a final stop at the Wind Cave. I found this otherworldly cavern vastly more interesting than the other Mulu caves that were open to the public. Ken and Franz's hats were blown off upon entering this cave; we now knew the origin of the cave's name.

Our foursome tiptoed our way along the boardwalks of this sub-terranean masterpiece, through a wide range of fantastic drippy "speleothem" resembling melted candle wax. Franz, the artist, insisted on pausing to do a quick oil pastel sketch of these wonders of nature. Jon began yet another round of uncontrollable sneezes.

Upon our return to the Melinau Canteen, we treated ourselves to icy cold soft drinks, followed by a much needed "mandi." Still dehydrated, that evening our foursome replenished our salt and satisfied our hunger with bags of salted peanuts while we recounted the events of the past few days.

Our band of four disparate backpackers discussed our future travel plans. Jon and I were each down to our last few Ringgit, in addition to the few days remaining on our visas. We needed to return to Kuching relatively soon, not to mention the fact that Jon's fire-damaged footwear now had a gaping hole. Franz and Ken had different plans. They were looking forward to head farther north into the Malaysian state of Sabah, and somehow travel overland to East Kalimantan within the Indonesian portion of Borneo.

DAY 22:

The four of us were drained from our adventure at Gunung Mulu National Park. Bleary eyed, we found ourselves drifting down a dark silent river at the predawn hour of 5:00 a.m. I flipped through my journal as the sun rose and reflected upon the past several weeks of comical adventures. My fellow travellers, whom I had met on the road, had provided an unending source of entertainment.

We finally arrived in the familiar town of Marudi. Strapping on our oversized backpacks, that we had thankfully done without over the past few days, we headed straight to our favorite Muslim restaurant.

After our final meal together, in typical backpacker fashion, we exchanged addresses, shook hands with beaming smiles, and wished our travel companions safe travels.

Franz and Ken, who were now bickering endlessly with one another, were now headed off together on their new adventure farther north into the Malaysian state of Sabah.

I reflected for a moment, and postulated that backpacking was an accelerated form of living. Compared to a "normal" sedentary lifestyle with a daily routine and a small circle of friends, life "on the road" seemed to produce multiple experiences and multiple intense relationships that would develop so quickly, they were often over in a matter of hours. Bidding our two cohorts farewell, Jon and I boarded an express boat bound for Miri.

Hours later, we disembarked in Miri and found ourselves back again at the familiar Miri Red Crescent Society. We were greeted by the same Punan family that seemed to have taken up permanent residence there.

That evening, after a filling meal at the Islamic Restaurant we had previously visited with the school teachers, Jon and I followed the sound of a distant rock band into a small club that we had overlooked during our last visit. An energetic Filipino band in matching costumes pounded out an impressive array of western tunes, which brought back memories of home.

At this sequestered nightspot, we struck up a conversation with the only other foreigner in the club: A heavy-set man drunkenly teetering on a stool at the end of the bar.

We soon invited Steve, an American oil worker, to join our table. He ended up buying us multiple rounds of beers as he had just been paid.

Like the other expat who had given us a lift from Lambir National Park, Steve was also living in Brunei, which he described as lacking a satisfactory level of nightlife. Like some other expats who resided there, he too would flee across the Malaysian border on the weekends and became inundated in the nefarious underworld of Miri.

As he continued to slur his words, he rubbed his bloated stomach while eyeing a table of giggling women and hiccuped. "Sorry guys, I've gotta go," he announced. He was kind enough to pay for our drinks before we returned to the Miri Red Crescent Society for one last night in this interesting border town.

DAY 23:
A random day of hitchhiking

09:03

After stopping by a morning Miri fruit market and stocking up on some exotic local fruit, we begin our long hike down the road to Bintulu ...

09:08

... Our first ride picks us up in just under five minutes -- what luck! Two truck drivers hauling tractor tires to the Miri airport. A short fifteen minute ride with a self-proclaimed drug addict ...

09:47

... Another truck, hauling a load of sand, screeches to a halt; the driver gives us a puzzled expression. His destination is Niah Town. We rumble onward for an hour before the truck overheats, stranding us near a rural farmhouse. We spend an unplanned thirty minute stop chatting with a roadside basket maker selling her wares ...

11:57

... After a successful repair, the sand truck driver continues on and dumps us off at a dry, dusty junction marked by a lone general store beneath a scorching sun. We seek refuge in the shade of the store and nibble on a few snacks to suffice as lunch. A passing truck driver stops by for a drink, and after buying him an icy Coca-Cola, he is happy to give us a ride!

12:23

... The driver guzzles down the Coke, as we board his truck hauling a shiny red sports car. We begin the journey to Bintulu down an atrocious pothole-filled road. An afternoon of intense rain showers bounce the cab back and forth violently for hours, as mud spatters across the windows.

16:44

... After thanking our driver profusely, we emerge from the truck upon reaching Bintulu. Regaining our balance, and extracting our packs -- now completely caked in mud -- from the rear of the truck, we trudge through town in search of accommodation ...

17:03

... We come across a ceremony at a Chinese temple, featuring dead pigs and goats with entrails exposed, displayed neatly on an altar. The attendees begin to light sticks of incense and wave them in symbolic patterns. Each smoldering stick of incense is then wedged into every orifice of these sacrificial creatures -- the nostrils, the ears, and the mouth ...

17:52

... We settle upon an unremarkable and cheap Bintulu guesthouse in which to spend the night. We take the remaining hours of the day to explore the restaurants and nightlife of this sprawling coastal town, as well as procuring schedules for buses headed to Sibu the following day.

DAY 24:

Jon and I awoke from a much needed long night of sleep; it seemed that we could never get enough sleep while on the road. We checked out of the guesthouse and prowled through Bintulu's darkened streets before sunrise. We found the 6 am bus to Sibu, and despite being the first bus of the day, it was already packed.

Jon and I paid the bus driver a few Ringgit and wedged our packs into a dangerously overcrowded vehicle that was headed southwest. A small pesky dog growled at a few captive chickens for the duration of our bumpy and uncomfortable four-hour journey. We stopped at every conceivable village, shuffling families and their goods in and out of the bus, throughout most of the morning.

By midday, we were enjoying our standard economical fare of roti canai and curry sauce in Sibu, as we patiently waited for a boat to Kuching.

As Jon repaired his boot with duct tape, we reminisced about the reverse journey that we had made from Kuching to Sibu by ship only three weeks earlier. On the speedy express boat back to Kuching, we found it remarkable that we had successfully travelled overland from Gunung Mulu to Kuching in the span of two and a half days without any advance preparation. We had wondered if the Dutch Duo could have made such a trip.

My mind drifted to the nagging mystery surrounding the purpose of my journey. I still had no idea of who had sent me the note ... or why.

Upon arrival in Kuching in the late afternoon, we rushed to reconfirm our flight booking back to Johor Bahru. We had heard the horror stories of overstaying one's visa from other travellers.

We found the airline ticketing office, and after peeling our almost illegible waterlogged flight tickets from the interior of our money belts, the agent shook her head and declared that our tickets were not valid for travel and she had no record of our reservations in her system. We howled with protest and explained our misadventures. After much pleading, she was kind enough to reissue our tickets and confirm our reservations.

"Do you know of any cheap places to stay?" asked Jon. The airline agent pointed us in the direction of some budget guesthouses, and we soon checked into a nameless lodging that appeared to double as some kind of warehouse.

We had almost come to the end of our journey in Borneo, as we both discussed what we would each do after reaching Singapore. I kept thinking: Had I just gone on a wild goose chase, returning to Hong Kong empty handed?

Before dinner, Jon spent a memorable hour trimming the scraggly beard he had grown over the past few weeks, leaving a comical Frank Zappa style moustache. Jon quipped, "They might think we're trouble-making hippies," as he purported that too much facial hair would result in certain detention by the immigration authorities. I followed suit ... just in case. We spent our final evening in Borneo at the Kuching night market and spent our few remaining Ringgit.

BUMBLING THROUGH BORNEO

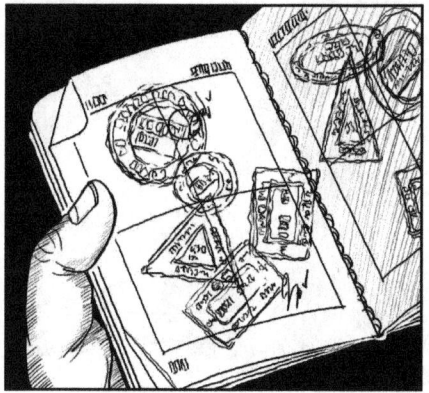 

DAY 25:

Jon and I hitched a ride to the Kuching airport in a blur of pre-dawn activities, and slept most of the 90-minute flight to Johor Bahru. Upon arrival in "JB" with our clean cut faces, we whizzed through a blur of immigration, leaving East Malaysia, entering Peninsular Malaysia, and then exiting almost immediately to neighboring Singapore -- all within the span of a couple of hours.

Jon and I decelerated from this day of travel and checked back in at Lee's Traveller's Hostel, the tiny Bencoolen Street guesthouse where Jon and I had met less than a month before.

Singapore proved to be one of those well-trodden crossroads of international budget travellers in this part of the world.

My Swedish travelling companion and I excitedly exchanged information and stories with other travellers. We were now a critical link in the "traveller's grapevine" for other independent travellers that were headed to Borneo.

I reflected upon this adventure and remembered my initial anticipation of hacking through jungles with a machete in search of fierce primitive headhunters deep in the heart of Borneo, only to be offered an icy Coca-Cola from a longhouse chief's refrigerator. I also remembered being overwhelmed by a place so rich in nature's treasures: primary rainforests teeming with innumerable species of plant and animal life, covering mammoth subterranean masterpieces, all formed over millions of years.

And all of this, bound together by fragile climatic and ecological systems that seemed to be quickly slipping out of balance. In a land of treasures, there always seemed to be treasure hunters. It seemed tragic that untold varieties of plant life and raw materials used in producing various medicinal products might be lost someday in the overcutting of the forests -- not to mention the spiritual value that the people of Sarawak had placed on this living entity. I pondered what would become of these treasures, as well as the myriad indigenous peoples clinging to their primitive origins, as they grapple with the economics of a growing country.

However, the real reason of my journey still evaded me. Why was I led to Borneo in the first place? And by whom? I had quite the adventure in this land of headhunters, but I certainly didn't find any tangible "great reward" up the Rejang River -- only a gift of a few local handicrafts from an obscure longhouse.

In fact, I had almost forgotten about those items. I dug the small package out of my backpack and withdrew the two exquisitely handcrafted items. Strangely, I had not even thought to open the tiny bamboo document holder ...

Could there be something inside? I held my breath and slowly twisted the cap. After inverting it, I was disappointed when nothing fell out. But upon closer inspection, there **was** something wedged inside!

I inserted the end of the hairpin into the tiny opening of the bamboo container and slowly slid out a tightly rolled piece of parchment. My heart pounding, I carefully unrolled the yellowing document.

I soon found two small scraps of paper rolled together. The larger of the two was torn around the edges and appeared to be a piece of a larger whole. The yellowing fabric-like parchment was covered by a series of hieroglyphic-like shapes that seemed vaguely familiar. Where had I seen this before? My heart skipped a beat when it finally dawned on me: This was the same Easter Island exhibit I had seen at the Sarawak Museum -- the one that had been withdrawn by its owner. My attention then shifted to the second smaller piece of paper. To my utter disbelief, scrawled in the same handwriting as my original note, was another cryptic message!

> SINGAPORE
>
> Poste Restante ...

My jaw dropped. This was unbelievable! Was Jim the Kayan behind this whole thing, despite only meeting him a few weeks ago? Was he the owner of the museum piece?

I thought it was strange that Jim had advised me to keep the small items a secret from my fellow travellers. Having already confided in Jon about the original note I received in Hong Kong, I nervously described to him what I had found. Why would I have been given such a rare historical find? Was it an accident?

Our curiosity got the best of us; Jon and I raced to Singapore's main post office. Would there be something for me there? Two nervous travellers arrived at the Poste Restante counter shortly before closing. My hair stood on end when there **was** a small packet bearing my name!

There was no return address; it had been mailed locally. I held the crumpled packet in my quivering hands and held it up to the light. Could this be the "reward?" I nervously glanced around.

Was I being set up? At a nearby table, I slowly opened the parcel. Inside was a wad of crisp banknotes and a single sheet of paper with yet another message written in the same handwriting:

> CHANGI YACHT CLUB
> Ask for Captain Dan...
>
> Guard the scroll with your life; it was not yet meant to be in a museum - you will soon understand...
>
> Discretion is of the utmost importance now...

I was dumbfounded. Where was Changi Yacht Club and who was Captain Dan? Upon quizzing the postal clerk, we discovered the Yacht Club was actually here in Singapore.

Was this scrap of parchment, or "scroll," the treasure that originally piqued my curiosity to travel here? It was obviously something of value.

After overhearing our query about the Yacht Club, we were cautiously approached by another backpacker who had been waiting behind us at the Poste Restante counter. Clutching a guidebook written in Japanese, he inquisitively produced a small note from a packet he had just retrieved, and held it up for us to see. It was **identical** to the one I had just received!

I gasped in shock and quickly showed him my matching note. He inhaled sharply, took two steps back and slowly howled with disbelief. He desperately tried to interrogate us; however, we didn't seem to have a common language.

Through a frantic game of charades and broken English, we were able to discern that this Japanese traveller, named Akira, had also received a mysterious package from an anonymous source in Tokyo. His note triggered a solo adventure through several obscure islands in the Philippines, before leading him to Singapore.

This was unbelievable. Who was responsible for these cryptic notes? It was clear I was not alone; this was far from a chance meeting. The money was real enough, and it appeared that a mysterious financial benefactor was keen to have us each press on ... but to where? And why?

I wondered if Akira had also found a similar matching piece of parchment, as evidenced by his note. Could I trust him? The note seemed to suggest otherwise. I surmised the parchment was torn from a larger whole. Perhaps that was the treasure! Were we both embroiled in an elaborate international treasure hunt of some kind? My mind raced with the possibilities.

My life in Hong Kong was virtually "on hold" enabling me to proceed with this madness, but Jon was at a crossroads. He was due to catch a flight to Australia the next morning, but the recent turn of events and the mysterious cash infusion gave him second thoughts.

Struggling to converse in broken English, Akira joined us as we drifted out of the post office into the humid equatorial air. Jon and Akira were both adamant that we follow the instructions on the note, find this alleged Captain Dan, and get to the bottom of this mystery. Were we all in some sort of trouble? It seems the adventure wasn't over yet ...

Our adrenalin pumping, our trio exchanged excited glances and hailed a passing taxi. I snapped, "Changi Yacht Club please!" as we scrambled into the back seat of the waiting taxi. In our rush getting into the vehicle, my new found envelope from the post office suddenly flipped out of my clumsy hands. Catching it in midair, to my horror, the inverted envelope sprayed a hefty amount of precious banknotes onto the sidewalk below!

The cab was already lurching forward as I hurriedly pulled in my legs and slammed the door. A crowd of pedestrians flocked to the rear of our departing taxi, excitedly snatching up the crisp banknotes fluttering in the wind as our trio of bumbling travellers squealed away from the curb and disappeared into a sea of Singaporean traffic.

> Follow the continuing misadventures of the Bumbling Travellers in
> **Volume 2:**
> **Bumbling Through Sumatra!**

BUMBLING TRAVELLER™ TRAVEL TIPS:

NOTICE TO TRAVELLERS:

This book is NOT intended for use as a travel guidebook for planning a trip to Borneo. The preceding story is based on travel to Borneo in the early 1990's; since that time, many places, modes of transportation, and means of access have changed significantly; please refer to the updates and resources listed below for more detailed information related to current events and travel planning.

TRAVEL UPDATES:

SINGAPORE ACCOMMODATION: Many of the Bencoolen Street hostels popular in the 1990s have since closed their doors.

SINGAPORE TO KUCHING: With the advent of low-cost airlines serving Singapore, flights to Kuching are no longer necessarily cheaper from Johor Bahru.

KUCHING: Road service from Kuching to Sibu is now relatively good, and overnight buses provide an economical means to travel between the two cities. Although there are regular ferries between Kuching and Sibu, the option for backpackers to economically travel from Kuching to Sibu via cargo ship has largely disappeared.

KAPIT TO BELAGA: Passenger boat travel through the dangerous Pelagus Rapids is no longer frequent or advisable for travellers.

MIRI TO BINTULU: The road connecting Niah Caves to each of these two cities has been vastly improved; the main Bintulu-Miri road near the Niah junction now boasts one of the best roadside hawker centers in Sarawak.

MIRI TO GUNUNG MULU: Travel between Miri and Gunung Mulu National Park is now typically by commuter plane; longboat travel has now become prohibitively expensive. Facilities and accommodation at Gunung Mulu National Park (and Camp 5) have been significantly upgraded. More and more caves are being surveyed each year, allowing for numerous opportunities for exploration.

THE KAYAN LONGHOUSE: The residents of the particular Kayan longhouse depicted in this book were forced to relocate to an alternate site due the construction of the Bakun Dam project. The longhouse is no longer accessible by travelers.

For updated travel information, consider checking Lonely Planet's Thorn Tree (www.lonelyplanet.com) for up-to-the minute information from fellow travellers.

BUMBLING TRAVELLER™ TRAVEL TIPS:

LEARN ABOUT THE COUNTRY:

• Remember that each country is unique and has different religious and social customs
• Learn as much of the local language as possible - the basics at a minimum
• Visit tourist information / visitor centers on arrival for local information
• Understand the political, social, and financial situation of the place in which you're travelling before you arrive

BEHAVIOR:
• Remember you are a guest in a foreign country; behave respectfully
• Make your trip a positive experience for both you and the people in the country you visit
• Dress and behave respectfully especially in religious and cultural areas
• Respect the dignity and privacy of others – ask before taking photos
• Observe local laws
• Avoid situations where you could be promoting human rights abuses
• Treat people the way you would like to be treated
• Don't work illegally or overstay your visa
• Avoid adversely affecting a culture by smoking in public -- better yet: quit smoking!
• Steer clear of drugs -- many countries carry the death penalty!
• Avoid buying illegal / banned products including tiger, leopard, and jaguar skins; turtles and tortoise shells; elephant ivory; meat of wild animals (bushmeat); orchids and cactii; reptile skins; and select kinds of caviar

BUMBLING TRAVELLER™ TRAVEL TIPS:

TRANSPORTATION:

• Travel in small groups, rather than large tours requiring a fleet of buses and large hotels

• Consider travelling in the off-season to avoid tourist crowds, but also be aware of inclement off-seasonal conditions that may exist at your destination

• Travel by land, and take public transportation whenever possible

• Minimize your air travel "carbon footprint" - take as few flights to your destination as possible; avoid intra-country air travel

• Choose environmentally responsible tour operators

• Travel using your own muscle-power if possible (walk, bike, paddle)

SUPPORT THE LOCALS:

• Respect indigenous peoples and traditional land owners; use indigenous vendors of services whenever possible

• Stay at locally owned and eco-friendly hotels and guesthouses whenever possible

• Eat where the locals eat

• Employ local people as guides; if hiring porters, don't ask them to carry a load that is too heavy for their physical abilities

• Purchase local "fair trade" products, arts and crafts made from sustainable materials; try to buy directly from the source / artisan

• Eat local rather than imported food

• Shop in local markets and mom & pop shops whenever possible

• Support local tour operators

• If you want to give money, support community projects rather than individuals

• Check to see if bargaining (haggling) for goods and services is acceptable in the culture you are visiting

• If the price is negotiable, pay a fair price so everyone wins

• Don't encourage begging by giving out money or candy

• Consider working as a volunteer in a community project

BUMBLING TRAVELLER™ TRAVEL TIPS:

MINIMIZE YOUR ENVIRONMENTAL IMPACT:

- Dispose of rubbish carefully (pack out your rubbish if trekking), recycle where possible, reuse your drink bottles and shopping bags
- Bring as few disposable products, and packaging as possible
- Minimize your use of water and energy
- Don't buy products made from coral, endangered plants or animals, or old growth trees
- Don't stand on, touch or remove any items from coral reefs
- Avoid disturbing wildlife and damaging their natural habitats
- Don't take any plants, rocks, or shells home with you
- Use only eco-friendly / biodegradable soaps
- Stay on designated trails whenever possible
- Take a shower rather than bath
- Leave a place as you found it
- Don't leave rubbish where wild animals might eat it
- Purify your own water (purification tablets or iodine) in your own water bottle instead of relying on bottled water
- If you need to poop in the bush, find a place 100 m. or farther from any watercourse, bury your poop (at least 20-30 cm. deep), and burn any toilet paper
- If bathing in rivers - follow the locals and bathe downstream from any water collection points
- Handwash your clothes whenever possible to avoid using washing machines

INTERNET RESOURCES:

Check out these online resources to learn more about current news, environmental, community, and travel / tourism issues in Sarawak:

NEWS:

Borneo Post	www.theborneopost.com
The Malaysia Star	http://thestar.com.my
New Straits Times	www.nst.com.my
The Malaysian Insider	www.themalaysianinsider.com
Malaysian National News Agency	www.bernama.com
Malaysiakini	www.malaysiakini.com

ENVIRONMENTAL ISSUES:

The Borneo Project	www.borneoproject.org
WWF-Malaysia	www.wwf.org.my
The Nature Conservancy	www.nature.org
Greenpeace	www.greenpeace.org
Malaysian Nature Society (MNS)	www.mns.org.my
Conservation International	www.conservation.org
Malaysian Timber Certification Council (MTCC)	www.mtcc.com.my
World Rainforest Movement	www.wrm.org
Rengah Sarawak	www.rengah.c2o.org
Natural Resources and Environment Board (NREB) Sarawak	www.nreb.gov.my
Green Assembly Asia	www.greenassembly.net
Wild Asia	www.wildasia.net
Planetsave	http://planetsave.com
Rainforest Portal	www.rainforestportal.org
Forest Protection Portal	http://forests.org
Forest Policy Research	http://forestpolicyresearch.org
Green Empowerment	http://www.greenempowerment.org/
Earth Island Institute	http://www.earthisland.org/
Mongabay.Com	http://www.mongabay.com/

INTERNET RESOURCES:

TRAVEL GUIDES:

Lonely Planet Travel Guides	www.lonelyplanet.com
Rough Guides	www.roughguides.com
Let's Go Travel Guides	www.letsgo.com
Moon Travel Guides	www.moon.com

RESPONSIBLE TOURISM / ECOTOURISM:

Tourism Malaysia	www.tourism.gov.my
World Tourism Organization	www.world-tourism.org
Pacific Asia Travel Association (PATA)	www.pata.org
Gunung Mulu National Park	www.mulupark.com
The Mulu Caves Project	www.mulucaves.org
Niah Caves	www.forestry.sarawak.gov.my
Transitions Abroad	www.transitionsabroad.com
Responsible Travel	www.responsible-travel.org
Ethical Traveler	www.ethicaltraveler.com
Survival International	www.survival-international.org
International Ecotourism Society	www.ecotourism.org
Tourism Concern	www.tourismconcern.org.uk
Sustainable Travel International (STI)	www.sustainabletravelinternational.org
Green Traveller	www.greentraveller.co.uk
Planeta.Com	www.planeta.com

OTHER RESOURCES:

Sarawak Dayak Iban Association (SADIA)	www.sadiakuching.org
Friend of the Earth Malaysia (Sahabat Alam Malaysia - SAM)	www.surforever.com/sam
Borneo Resources Institute (BRIMAS)	http://brimas.www1.50megs.com

DISCLAIMER: The above resources are provided for information only; the author and publisher accept no responsibility for the content of third-party websites.

About the Author:

Tom Schmidt is an award-winning architect, writer, illustrator, musician, and part-time stand-up comedian.

Born in the United States, following his studies of Architecture and Environmental Design at the University of Colorado, his wanderlust has carried him through various bumbling adventures in more than 70 countries around the world and across all seven continents.

Schmidt is a licensed architect in the USA and New Zealand, an Accredited Professional in the LEED and WELL building certification programs, a founding member of the Hong Kong Chapter of the American Institute of Architects (AIA), and a member of the American Society of Architectural Illustrators (ASAI).

Schmidt is the Founder and Managing Director of *Sepia Design Consultants Limited*, a hospitality design consultancy.
www.sepiadesign.com

He has resided in Hong Kong since 1997.

 **Bumbling Through Borneo** is Volume 1 in the Bumbling Traveller™ Adventure Series, a book series that seeks to promote environmental and cultural awareness through entertaining mysteries and adventures.

CHECK OUT THE OTHER VOLUMES IN THE AWARD-WINNING BUMBLING TRAVELLER™ ADVENTURE SERIES!

VOLUME 2: BUMBLING THROUGH SUMATRA
by Tom Schmidt
ISBN 978-988-18066-6-6

Follow the humorous day-to-day antics of Bumbling Bob, a wayward American architect, on his continuing quest across the Indonesian island of Sumatra with a ragtag troupe of bumbling backpackers. Share a harrowing nautical sojourn through the pirate-infested waters of the Strait of Malacca, misadventures in ports along Malaysia's west coast, and an arduous overland journey across Sumatra ending with a mystical encounter with the shamans of the indigenous tribes of the Mentawai Islands. Discover Sumatra -- a land rich in ancient treasures whose fate teeters in the environmental balance!

- **Bronze Medal Winner** - Independent Publishers Book Awards

VOLUME 3: BUMBLING THROUGH HONG KONG
by Tom Schmidt
ISBN 978-988-18066-7-3

Follow the continuing illustrated daily antics of Bumbling Bob, a wayward American architect entrusted to carry a mysterious treasure, on his random travels throughout the Pearl of the Orient with a ragtag troupe of backpackers. Share a fast-paced adventure through one of the most densely inhabited population centers on the planet, and a series of educational discoveries while the bumbling travellers search for an elusive doctor who holds the key to a lingering mystery. Discover Hong Kong -- a land rich in natural assets and cultural treasures whose fate teeters in the environmental balance!

- **Silver Medal Winner** - Moonbeam Children's Book Awards
- **Bronze Medal Winner** - Independent Publishers Book Awards

AVAILABLE AT BOOKSTORES
OR ORDER ONLINE AT **WWW.KAKIBUBU.COM**
PayPal / credit cards accepted

www.ingramcontent.com/pod-product-compliance
Lightning Source LLC
Chambersburg PA
CBHW060844050426
42453CB00008B/825